The MAGIC of OUR WORLD

From the Night Sky to the Pacific Islands
with Favorite Disney Characters

Lerner Publications • Minneapolis

CONTENTS

THE MAGIC AROUND US

The world has so much for us to discover! Moana explored the land and waters around the spectacular Pacific Islands. Dory journeyed across the vast ocean and saw more than a few wonders. Anna and Elsa gazed at colorful lights shining in the sky above Arendelle. And Lightning McQueen showed the power of cars during his incredible races. Discover more about this amazing world, from the ocean to the sky and everything in between. There is plenty of magic all around. Come and take a look!

CHAPTER 1

The Night Sky

WONDERS IN THE SKY

Have you ever been curious about the amazing things we see in the night sky? Olaf and his friends have! Let's explore the wonders of the night sky together!

Day and Night

Do you know why day turns into night? It's because our planet is always spinning. Earth makes one full spin on its axis every twenty-four hours. The side facing the sun experiences day. The side facing away from the sun experiences night.

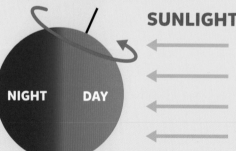

EARTH

SUNLIGHT

NIGHT   DAY

AXIS

SUN

Celestial Bodies

Celestial bodies are objects in space that we can see in our sky. The sun, moon, and stars are all celestial bodies. Which celestial bodies have you seen during the day? Which have you seen at night? Are there any that you've seen during the day *and* night?

The Day Sky

The sun is the closest star to Earth. During the day, the sun's light is so bright that we can't see any other stars. But we often see the sun shining in a blue sky.

The Night Sky

At night, we can see more celestial bodies than we can during the day. We can often see the moon and stars. Sometimes we might see planets like Venus and Jupiter.

THE NORTHERN LIGHTS

When Anna was very young, she'd tell Elsa, "The sky's awake, so I'm awake, so we have to play!" What do you think Anna meant? Let's find out!

The Aurora

What makes the sky look awake to Anna? The beautiful colors that light up the dark! What's going on? Something amazing called the aurora. The aurora can have many colors and shapes. Sometimes it is hard to see. Other times the whole sky is bright.

Aurora Borealis

The aurora seen from northern parts of Earth is called the northern lights. Usually the farther north you go, the better your chances of seeing these colorful lights. Scientists have a special name for the northern lights. They call them the aurora borealis.

NORTH POLE

EQUATOR

SOUTH POLE

Anna and Elsa play in the castle. Outside, lights dance in the night sky. Arendelle is a magical place!

WHAT CAUSES THE NORTHERN LIGHTS?

When Anna and Elsa were children, their parents took them on a trip. They went to the top of a tall mountain to watch the northern lights. Elsa used her magical powers to make a staircase out of snow. The sisters felt as if they were running into the colorful sky.

Solar Energy

But what causes the colorful northern lights? The answer starts with the sun. The sun is full of energy. That energy travels to Earth and gives us light and heat. Some of the sun's energy is made up of tiny specks called electrons.

Atmospheric
Gases

Earth is covered in an atmosphere. The atmosphere is a thin layer of gases including nitrogen and oxygen. These gases are the air that we breathe. There's no air in outer space. Earth's atmosphere keeps us alive!

OUTER SPACE

EARTH'S ATMOSPHERE

(nitrogen, oxygen, and other gases)

Sparks!
Flashes!

The electrons from the sun hit the gases in our atmosphere. Sometimes when they hit each other, the crash makes a spark. This spark can be a flash of color. If there are a lot of these crashes when the sky is dark and clear, we can see them. Can you guess what they are called? That's right: the aurora!

EXPLORING THE AURORA

You never forget the first time you see the northern lights. Olaf saw them on the night Elsa made him with her magic! The sky filled with wiggling, glowing green lights. What a sight!

All the Different Colors

The aurora comes in different colors. It depends on which gas from the atmosphere hits the sun's electrons. Crashes with oxygen are usually green. These are the most common. Sometimes they can also be red. Crashes with nitrogen are mostly blue. The colors can blend together too. That's why you can sometimes see purple, white, and even pink lights.

RAYS

BANDS

CORONA

All the Different Shapes

The aurora can also appear in different shapes. They ripple, pulse, glow, and make trails. They can look like curtains. They can look like blobs. They can look like waves. Scientists give the different shapes names, like rays, bands, and corona. Why are they so different from each other? Scientists aren't totally sure. It may have to do with how the electrons crash into the gases in the atmosphere. One thing we do know: they look amazing!

TROLLS, CRYSTALS, AND OTHER STORIES

Many cultures have created stories to explain the northern lights. Olaf is curious about these stories. Are you? Let's learn about some of these stories together!

Kristoff knows about the troll crystals of Arendelle. They give off a special glow. Sometimes the crystals start to go dark. Then they have to be recharged before the northern lights lose their color!

Fox Fire

The people of Finland have a story about the northern lights. They say the lights come from a fox made of fire. The fox runs on the snow into the Far North. When the fox sweeps its tail, sparks fly up into the sky. That's why they call the northern lights "fox fire."

The Valkyries

There are myths from Norway about female spirits called Valkyries. These warrior maidens watched over soldiers in battle. Some people believed the northern lights were reflections off the armor and shields of the Valkyries.

Herring Flash

In ancient Sweden, the aurora was called "herring flash." A herring is a tiny fish with bright scales. People believed the aurora was the light bouncing off these fish swimming in the sea. Seeing the herring flash meant they were about to catch a lot of fish.

SCIENCE IN ARENDELLE

In Elsa's time, people were beginning to understand the northern lights. It has taken us a long time to learn the facts. And there is still a lot more to learn! Let's find out what scientists used to think about the northern lights.

Magnetic Fields

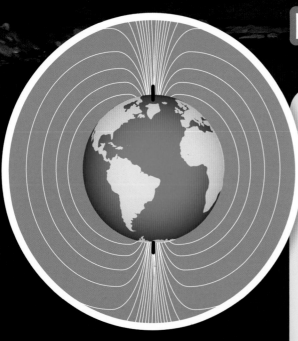

Scientists have known for many years that Earth is a giant magnet. Earth's magnetic field affects the energy all around us. Scientists realized early on that this magnetic field had something to do with the northern lights. And they were right! The power of the magnet at the poles draws electrons from the sun.

Looking for Patterns

Scientists spend a lot of time looking and listening and measuring. They studied the northern lights for many years. They were looking for patterns. When something happens over and over, it helps us learn about it. But the northern lights are hard to study. They are very unpredictable.

A telescope from Anna and Elsa's time

A Closer Look

Scientists use telescopes to get a closer look at objects in the sky. Telescopes are tools that make distant objects appear bigger and clearer. In the last two hundred years, telescopes have gotten much more powerful. Today we even have telescopes in space! These telescopes produce images that would have amazed scientists in Anna and Elsa's time.

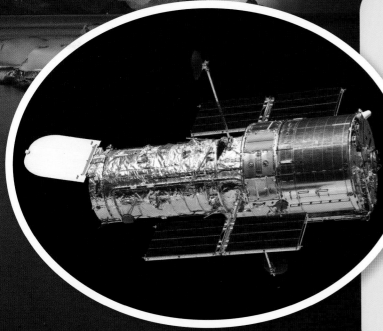

Hubble Space Telescope

WHERE CAN I SEE THE LIGHTS?

Anna, Elsa, and Olaf have special memories of the northern lights. So do Kristoff and Sven! The question is, Where can you go to see these beautiful lights?

Show Me the Lights!

Where exactly can we see the northern lights on Earth? Northern countries like Sweden, Norway, and Finland are great places to look for them. Alaska and northern Canada often have good views too. You could also try Greenland, Iceland, or northern Russia. The closer you get to the North Pole, the easier they are to see.

Polar Lights

The north isn't the only place you can see the aurora. You can also see auroras in the south. Those are called the southern lights. The farther you get from the equator, the more likely you are to see auroras! The northern lights and southern lights are also called the polar lights.

NORTHERN LIGHTS

EQUATOR

SOUTHERN LIGHTS

Aurora Australis

The southern lights have another name. They are called the aurora australis. They can be seen from New Zealand, Australia, South America, and Antarctica. As with the northern lights, the closer you are to the pole, the better your view!

COLD PLACES

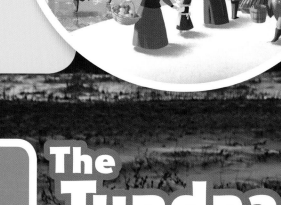

Arendelle is a beautiful kingdom. There is a castle and a town. There are fjords, forests, and mountains. It gets very cold there in the winter. Parts of the kingdom are tundras. What do you know about the tundra?

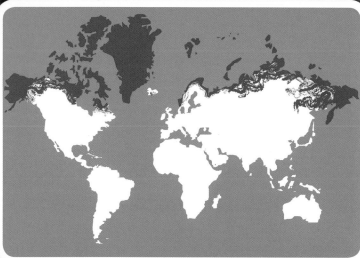

The Tundra

The tundra is a very cold region with very few trees. Winters last a long time in the tundra. Summers are short. Some tundra regions are located high in the mountains. The purple areas in this map are tundras.

People

Few people live in the Arctic. But one group of people has lived in Arctic regions for thousands of years. They are called the Sami people. They live in parts of Norway, Sweden, Finland, and Russia. Traditionally, they have made a living by fishing and by herding reindeer.

Animals

Lots of animals live in the tundra. These include owls, foxes, wolves, and reindeer. Foxes and reindeer have thick fur that protects them from the cold. Arctic wolves have fur on their paws that gives them a better grip on the icy ground. Some animals, like huskies, even help people get around! These dogs are very strong and can pull sleds for a long time.

Plants

What kinds of plants grow in the tundra? Short ones! It's so cold and windy that big plants have trouble surviving. But there are a lot of small plants like mosses and shrubs!

WHEN TO WATCH THE LIGHTS

Anna and Elsa love to watch the northern lights. So do their friends. But it's not enough for them to be in the right place. It also has to be the right time! Let's learn about the best time to watch the northern lights.

What Time of Day?

The skies have to be dark to see the northern lights. Otherwise, sunlight will block them out. In the Far North, it can get dark very early in the winter. Some people think the best time to see the aurora is between 9:30 p.m. and 1:30 a.m. That's pretty late!

What Time of Year?

Winter is the best time to see the northern lights. Why is that? Because the sun sets earlier and rises later. In some northern regions, you can see the aurora as early as 4 p.m.! Winter nights in the north are long and dark. This makes it easier to see the northern lights.

The Solar Cycle

Our sun has a magnetic field, just like Earth. Every eleven years, the sun's magnetic activity is very high. This is called the solar maximum. This is the best time to see the auroras because it's when the sun's energy is the strongest. The auroras are very active for two years before and two years after the solar maximum.

WHAT CAUSES THE SEASONS?

Do you know what Olaf's favorite season is? It's summer! Do you know why we have different seasons? Keep reading to find out!

SPRING

SUMMER

SUN

WINTER

FALL

Earth's Tilt

We experience different seasons because Earth is tilted. The tilt of the Earth changes how much sunlight gets to different parts of Earth. When the northern part of Earth is close to the sun, it's warmer there. That is summer. When the sun is farther from the northern part of Earth, it's colder there. That is winter. In between, we have fall and spring.

Hemispheres and Seasons

Winter does not happen at the same time all over the world. The bottom half of Earth has opposite seasons from the top half. When it's summer in the Northern Hemisphere, it's winter in the Southern Hemisphere.

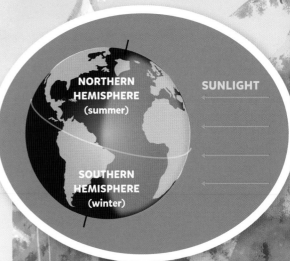

NORTHERN HEMISPHERE (summer)

SOUTHERN HEMISPHERE (winter)

SUNLIGHT

SPRING | **SUMMER**

FALL | **WINTER**

Seasonal Weather

Have you noticed changes in the weather as seasons change? Maybe it's cold and snowy in winter but warm and rainy in spring. Summer might be hot and sunny, while fall is cool and windy. These changes are related to Earth's tilt and the path our planet travels around the sun.

Dressing for the Weather

When it's cold out, it's very important to stay warm! A good way to do this is to cover as much skin as you can. Wearing a jacket, gloves, scarf, and hat will help. Anna found warm clothes at Oaken's Trading Post when Elsa created a snowstorm during summer. Can you point out all the items that help her stay warm?

DAYLIGHT AND NIGHTFALL

Anna, Elsa, and their friends love to go on adventures! Not all their adventures happen during the day. Sometimes they find themselves out at night. How much do you know about night and day?

Midnight Sun

The farther north or south you get, the more Earth's tilt matters. In the Far North, the sun is so high in the sky during summer that it doesn't always fully set. This is called the midnight sun. The same is true in the Far South.

Polar Night

In the winter, the opposite is true! The sun is so low that it's dark for long stretches of time. This is called polar night. Around the equator, the sun is always high in the sky. It stays fairly warm year-round. And the time of sunrises and sunsets doesn't change much.

Solstices and Equinoxes

In many countries, the summer solstice is the first day of summer. It's the longest day of the year! The winter solstice is the shortest day of the year. It marks the first day of winter in many places. The days and nights are of similar lengths during the fall and spring. It's called an equinox when day and night are exactly the same length. There are two of those—one in the fall and one in the spring.

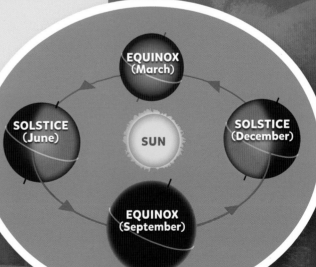

LATE-NIGHT STARGAZING

Looking at the night sky can be really fun! Kristoff sings a song for Olaf, Anna, Elsa, and Sven. The friends enjoy the music as the northern lights dance above.

When the Sun Goes Down

You can't see the stars until the sun sets. The sun goes down at different times throughout the year. In the summer, you might have to stay up late to see the sun go down. The sun sets very early in winter, especially in the Far North.

What to Bring

You might want to bring a few things with you when you go stargazing. Make sure you dress warmly! If you're going to lie down on the ground, you might like a blanket to lie on. Binoculars can help you see things in the night sky. Another helpful tool is a flashlight covered with red cellophane. This will help you see in the dark without ruining your night vision.

Get Some Sleep!

As fun as it is to stargaze, it's also really important to get a good night's sleep. Kids need about ten hours of sleep every night. If you do stay up after dark to look at the stars, make sure you can sleep late the next day. Sleep is important. Just ask Kristoff!

THE STARS IN THE SKY

On a clear night, we can see thousands of stars in the sky. During the day, we can see only one: our sun! Olaf loves feeling the warmth of the sun's rays. Let's learn more about our sun and other stars.

What Are Stars?

What exactly are stars? They're giant spheres of hot gas. They create huge amounts of energy. They're like power plants! We experience our sun's energy as light and heat. Stars can live for billions of years. They are different sizes and even different colors. The coolest stars are red. The hottest stars are white or blue. Even the coolest star is very hot.

Our  Sun

Our sun is the closest star to Earth. Earth orbits around the sun. It takes a year for Earth to travel around the sun one time. Here are some sun facts that may amaze you. The sun is 93 million miles (150 million km) away from us. It is 4.5 billion years old. The center of the sun is 27 million degrees Fahrenheit (15 million degrees C). Wow, that's hot!

Galaxies

Giant groups of stars are called galaxies. Stars usually spin aroun the center of their galaxy, just as Earth spins around the sun. Many galaxies are shaped like spirals.

The Milky Way

We are in a spiral galaxy called the Milky Way. There are at least one hundred billion stars in the Milky Way. It takes our sun more than two hundred million years to orbit around the center of the galaxy. What we can see of our galaxy from Earth looks like a milky band across the sky. That's why ancient people called it the Milky Way.

NAVIGATING
BY THE STARS

Arendelle has a strong tradition of sailing. Maps and compasses can help people sail from one place to another. But did you know that stars can also help sailors navigate? Let's find out how!

The North Star

Many sailors use the North Star to help them navigate. Navigation means figuring out where you are and where you want to go. The North Star is a bright star seen in the Northern Hemisphere. Its scientific name is Polaris. The stars "move" in the sky as Earth rotates, but the North Star stays in the same place. This photo was taken over many hours. Can you find the North Star?

Constellations

A constellation is a group of stars that form a shape in the sky. Throughout history, travelers have used constellations to help them navigate. Many constellations are named after animals. Some are named after people or mythical creatures. Have you heard of the Big Dipper? It is part of a constellation called Ursa Major, or "Great Bear." The two stars at the end of the dipper point directly at the North Star. The North Star is part of the constellation called the Little Dipper.

LITTLE DIPPER

POLARIS (NORTH STAR)

BIG DIPPER

The Southern Cross

SOUTHERN CROSS

points toward the SOUTH CELESTIAL POLE

The North Star can be seen only in the Northern Hemisphere. What if you are south of that? In the Southern Hemisphere, travelers use a constellation called the Southern Cross to help them navigate. The long bar of the cross points to the south celestial pole. This is the point in the sky directly above the South Pole.

DISCOVERING THE PLANETS

Where does Olaf live? Arendelle! Olaf loves learning everything about his home. How well do you know your town? Your country? Your planet?

SATURN

NEPTUNE

Planets

What are planets? We're on one right now! Planets are large bodies that orbit around a star. Our planet, Earth, orbits around the sun. Some planets, like Earth, are made of rock and dirt. Other planets are made of gas. Saturn is one example. Uranus and Neptune are made of both gas and ice.

The Solar System

All the planets that orbit our sun are part of the solar system. There are eight planets plus some dwarf planets. The closest planet to the sun is Mercury. Mercury travels around the sun in only eighty-eight days. The farthest planet is Neptune. It takes Neptune 165 years to travel around the sun! Pluto is one of the dwarf planets. It's too small to be a full planet. It's even farther away from the sun than Neptune!

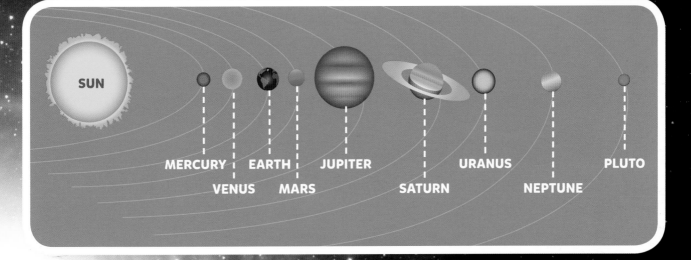

SUN

MERCURY · EARTH · JUPITER · URANUS · PLUTO

VENUS · MARS · SATURN · NEPTUNE

The Planet We Call Home

Earth is the third planet from the sun. As far as we know, it's the only planet in the solar system that can support life. The other planets don't have air that we can breathe. They are also either too hot or too cold.

THE MOON

When Anna met Prince Hans, she thought she had found true love. Hans turned out to be a villain. But Anna still remembers how bright and beautiful the moon was that night.

Meet Our Moon

A moon is an object that orbits a planet. Some planets have many moons. Our planet has one. Our moon orbits Earth about every twenty-seven days. Have you noticed that the moon changes shape? Sometimes it looks like a circle in the sky. Sometimes it's half a circle. Sometimes we can't see it at all! What is going on? It has to do with where the moon is when the sun shines on it.

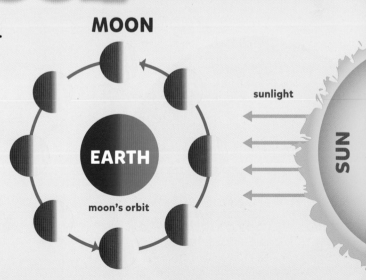

MOON

EARTH

moon's orbit

sunlight

SUN

Phases of the Moon

The different shapes of the moon we see are called phases. When Earth is between the moon and the sun, we can see a full moon. When the moon is between the sun and Earth, the moon is invisible. This is called a new moon. In between these phases, it can be a crescent moon, a gibbous moon, or a quarter moon. So many phases!

NEW MOON	CRESCENT MOON	QUARTER MOON	GIBBOUS MOON	FULL MOON	GIBBOUS MOON	QUARTER MOON	CRESCENT MOON

The Far Side of the Moon

Did you know that the same side of the moon always faces Earth? This is because the moon turns at just the right speed as it orbits Earth. Have you heard the expression "the dark side of the moon"? There actually isn't a dark side of the moon. All parts of the moon get sunlight. We just can't see the far side from Earth.

ECLIPSES

What follows you around everywhere you go? Your shadow! Shadows are made when light can't shine through something. People have shadows. Objects have shadows. Even snowmen have shadows. Just look at Olaf!

What Is an Eclipse?

Earth and the moon have shadows too. What happens when an object in space moves into the shadow of another object? An eclipse. On Earth, there are two kinds of eclipses. They both involve the sun and the moon. Let's learn about them!

Solar Eclipse

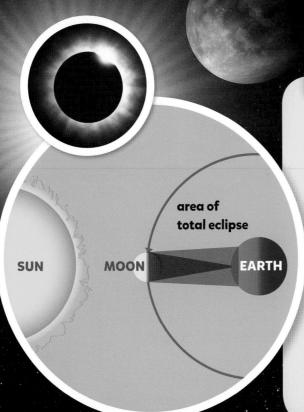

area of total eclipse

SUN · MOON · EARTH

Solar eclipses happen when the moon gets between Earth and the sun. They occur once every eighteen months. A total solar eclipse happens when the sun, the moon, and Earth are in a straight line. If you're in the right place, the sun will go dark—and so will the sky! Solar eclipses last only for a few minutes. Never look right at a solar eclipse. It can harm your eyes.

Lunar Eclipse

A lunar eclipse happens when Earth gets between the sun and the moon. The moon is in Earth's shadow. We can still see the moon during a total lunar eclipse. Why is that? Because some light gets bent by Earth's atmosphere and hits the moon. The moon looks red during a lunar eclipse.

SUN · EARTH · MOON

COMETS AND METEORS

Anna loves to look at the night sky. There are so many wondrous things to see. There are stars, planets, the moon, and even the northern lights! Anna never gets tired of looking up. Is that a shooting star? Let's find out.

Comets

There's a lot more to space than planets, stars, and moons. Do you know about comets? Comets are big balls made mostly of ice. They are too small to be planets. They orbit around stars and have tails that we can see in the sky. The tails are made from the ice heated by the sun and turned into a gas.

Meteoroids, Meteors, and Meteorites

Meteoroids are rocks in space. Sometimes these rocks hit Earth. As they travel through our atmosphere, they often burn up and turn into dust. When they burn, we can see a streak of light. This is called a meteor. Sometimes the rock doesn't completely burn up. Some of it makes it to the ground. The part that lands is called a meteorite.

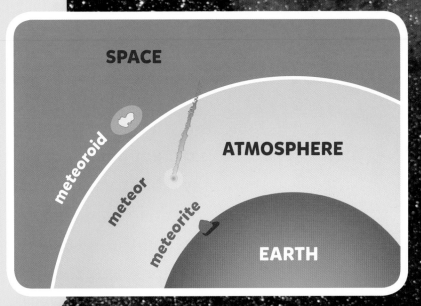

SPACE

meteoroid

meteor

meteorite

ATMOSPHERE

EARTH

What Are Shooting Stars?

Have you ever seen a shooting star? Did you know that shooting stars aren't actually stars at all? They're meteors! Thousands of meteors streak through Earth's sky every day. Sometimes Earth passes through an area where a comet once traveled. Comets can leave a trail of dust behind them. When Earth moves through this trail, it can create a meteor shower. This is when we can see lots of meteors in a single night.

BEST VIEWING CONDITIONS

Anna and Elsa are lucky. Arendelle is a great place to look at the night sky! The stars shine bright, and the northern lights glow. Let's learn about the best conditions for seeing things in the night sky.

Cloudy or Clear?

Sometimes it can be cloudy at night. Clouds can make it hard to see the stars and even the moon. The best time to go stargazing is on a clear night. Then you might even see a meteor or two!

Light Pollution

A dark sky is just as important as a clear sky. The darker it is, the more you can see! If you live in a city, you might have to deal with light pollution. Light pollution means that the lights on Earth are so bright that they block out the light of the stars. A full moon can also add to light pollution. The light from the full moon is so bright that it can make it hard to see many stars.

Outside the City

If you can get away from the glow of city lights, you can see so much more in the night sky. In a city, you might be able to see only ten stars. On a clear night far from city lights, you can see about twenty-five hundred stars in the sky! The longer you look, the more your eyes get used to the dark. This means you can see even more stars.

KEEP ON EXPLORING

With the help of Anna, Elsa, Olaf, Kristoff, and Sven, we've learned so much about the night sky! We know about the northern lights and the stars and planets that light up our night sky. But there is always more to explore. Now it's your turn to take what you know and go look at the night sky. Plan a stargazing night with family and friends. Sharing the beauty of the night sky can be a magical experience!

CHAPTER 2

THE OCEAN WORLD

The ocean is an amazing place. It is full of marvelous creatures . . . like Dory! Let's discover the ocean that Dory and her friends call home.

WELCOME TO THE OCEAN!

SO MUCH OCEAN!

More than 70 percent of our planet is ocean. The ocean is home to more than a million animals and plants. The water in rivers and lakes is fresh water. The water in the ocean is salty!

Arctic

Pacific

Atlantic

Pacific

Indian

Southern

OCEAN HABITATS

The ocean is a big place. Some parts of the ocean are warm. Some parts are cold. Ocean floors have mountains and valleys and even forests made of kelp! Different parts of the ocean are home to many different creatures.

BLUE TANGS

Dory is a blue tang. Blue tangs are saltwater fish that live in coral reefs and rock-filled waters close to shore. Blue tangs can't survive in the cold. They usually stay in warm parts of the ocean.

Let's meet some of Dory's underwater friends! Look, there's Nemo, Destiny, and Mr. Ray . . . and is that Hank too?

WATER-BREATHING OCEAN ANIMALS

WHALE SHARKS

Do you know that Destiny is a whale shark? Whale sharks live in the warmer oceans of the world. They live near the surface, but they are able to dive thousands of feet under the water.

OCTOPUSES

Octopuses like Hank live in all the oceans of the world. There are over three hundred kinds of octopuses! Many of them live in shallow water. Octopuses have eight legs . . . and three hearts!

CLOWN FISH

Nemo is a clown fish.
Clown fish live in coral reefs.
There are twenty-eight kinds
of clown fish! They grow to
about 4 inches
(10 cm) long.

RAYS

Mr. Ray is a spotted eagle ray.
Eagle rays live in warm, shallow
water near the coast. Rays hunt for
clams, crabs, sea urchins, octopuses,
and squid on the ocean floor.
Their eyes are on top of
their heads.

Not all of Dory's friends are fish. (Just look at Hank!) Dory is friends with all kinds of animals. Some of them live under the water, and some live on the ocean's surface. Say hello to Bailey, Crush, and Squirt. Oh! Here are Fluke and Rudder too!

AIR-BREATHING OCEAN ANIMALS

BELUGA WHALES

Dory's friend Bailey is a beluga whale. Beluga whales live in the cold water of the Far North. Beluga whales are mammals, not fish. Fish breathe by taking oxygen out of the water, have cold blood, and many lay eggs. Mammals breathe air to get oxygen, have warm blood, and even have hair. Beluga whales usually swim just under the surface of the ocean. This way they can come up to the surface to breathe air whenever they need it!

SEA LIONS

Fluke and Rudder are California sea lions. California sea lions live along the coast of the Pacific Ocean. They are at home on land and in the water. They spend most of their days above water lying on rocks, but they are amazing swimmers. They can even sleep in the water!

SEA TURTLES

Squirt and his dad, Crush, are sea turtles. Sea turtles have been swimming in the oceans since the time of the dinosaurs! Sea turtles can be found all over the world. They come up to the surface to breathe. They can hold their breath underwater for hours at a time!

Dory and her friends have something in common. They all breathe oxygen. Fish like Dory and Nemo get oxygen from the water. Octopuses like Hank do too. Mammals like Fluke and Bailey get oxygen from the air. So do reptiles like Crush and Squirt. And so do we!

HOW DIFFERENT SEA CREATURES GET OXYGEN

GILLS

Fish have gills next to their mouths. Gills are what let fish breathe underwater. The fish takes in a mouthful of water and pushes the water out through its gills. As the water flows through the gills, the gills take oxygen from the water for the fish to breathe. Octopuses have gills too, even though they are not fish.

HOLD YOUR BREATH

Mammals such as whales and sea lions can hold their breath for a really long time. This is so they can dive for food without needing to come up for air. Sometimes Bailey or Fluke go on deep dives. They can even slow down their hearts so that the oxygen in their lungs lasts a lot longer.

BLOWHOLES

Whales like Bailey have blowholes on top of their heads. Blowholes are like whale nostrils. Beluga whales come to the surface to breathe out—and take in a breath of fresh air—through their blowholes. When a beluga is underwater, it keeps its blowhole closed so water cannot get in.

Some animals can live on the land AND in the water. We call these animals amphibious. Dory's friends Fluke and Rudder are both amphibians. So is Becky the loon!

AMPHIBIOUS ANIMALS

FLIPPING FLIPPERS

See those big back flippers? They flip forward and become little feet when sea lions are on land. This lets them walk on all fours! It is a great example of an amphibian adaptation. A sea lion's back flippers are useful on land and in the water!

SUPER SWIMMERS

California sea lions are incredible swimmers! They normally swim along at 11 miles (18 km) per hour but can swim in bursts of up to 25 miles (40 km) per hour. That's pretty fast for an animal that can weigh 860 pounds (390 kg)! They can dive almost 1,000 feet (300 m) under the water, holding their breath the whole time.

LOONS

Loons are also amphibious. They are birds that live on the water. Loons are fast swimmers and even faster fliers! They can hold their breath for a long time. This lets them dive in the water to catch fish.

Some mammals breathe air but spend their whole lives in the ocean, like Dory's friend Bailey the beluga whale! Let's meet some other ocean animals that are like Bailey. These are warm-blooded mammals that never set foot on land.

NON-AMPHIBIOUS ANIMALS

SPERM WHALES

Meet the sperm whale! Sperm whales have huge brains. Their brains weigh almost 20 pounds (9 kg)! Sperm whales have teeth. They use their teeth to eat squid, fish, and octopuses. They live all over the world. They usually live in groups called pods.

DOLPHINS

Dolphins are some of the smartest animals in the world! Like beluga whales, dolphins live in the ocean but must go to the surface to breathe air. Just like whales, dolphins have blowholes on top of their heads. Dolphins live in most of the world's oceans.

BLUE WHALES

The blue whale is the largest animal on the planet. That includes land animals! They can be as big as 100 feet (30 m) long and weigh 160 tons (145 t). Blue whales have two blowholes and no teeth. They live all over the world. Unlike beluga whales and dolphins, they usually live alone.

Not all animals spend their whole lives in the same place. Just ask Dory and Nemo! But some kinds of animals actually make long journeys every year. This is called migration. Nemo's teacher, Mr. Ray, knows all about migration. Let's learn about it!

MIGRATION

WHY DO ANIMALS MIGRATE?

There are a few reasons why some ocean animals migrate every year. The big reason is to find food. Some animals migrate to head for warmer waters. Some animals migrate when they are ready to have babies.

MIGRATION PATTERNS

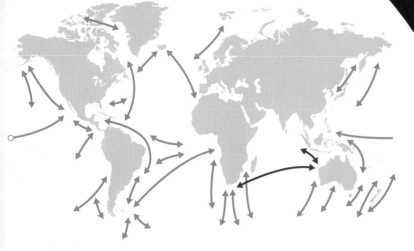

● GRAY WHALES, HUMPBACK WHALES, SOUTHERN RIGHT WHALES
● WHALE SHARKS, GREAT WHITE SHARKS
● LEATHERBACK TURTLES, GREEN TURTLES

WHALE MIGRATION

Beluga whales also migrate. Beluga whales live in the cold waters of the Far North. They travel south every fall to avoid the ice. They need to get to warmer waters before the northern waters start to freeze. One group travels more than 3,000 miles (4,800 km) . . . each way!

STINGRAY MIGRATION

A large group of stingrays is called a fever.

One type of ray is the stingray. A stingray migration is a magical sight. Twice a year, these normally solitary fish gather in huge groups and travel hundreds of miles! Why do they do this? We're not sure. We think it's probably to go to new feeding grounds.

Bailey is a beluga whale, and Destiny is a whale shark . . . so they must be the same kind of animal, right? Actually, they're very different! Whale sharks are fish. Beluga whales are whales, and whales are mammals. Let's discover some of the differences between fish and whales.

WHALES VS. FISH

ECHOLOCATION

Echolocation is a way that toothed whales like Bailey use sound to find and measure the shapes of things, just as we use our eyes. It helps whales get around! Here's how it works. Beluga whales make a clicking sound. That sound bounces off everything around them. Some clicks bounce back toward the whale, and the beluga listens for the echo. Whales can tell a lot about their environment from the echo!

BLUBBER

BELUGA WHALE

BLUBBER

NO BLUBBER

FISH

Under their skin, whales are covered from head to tail in blubber. Blubber is a thick layer of fat. It keeps whales warm in the cold ocean. Whales are warm-blooded mammals like us. They need the extra layer of fat to stay warm! So why don't fish have blubber? It's because fish are cold-blooded—their blood is the same temperature as the water around them.

THE TAIL FIN

Take a look at the tail fins of the whale shark and the beluga whale. Whale sharks, like all fish, have vertical tails. But whales have horizontal tails called flukes. That's because fish move their tails side to side, while whales move their tails up and down!

Let's find out how Dory and her friends move around. We call this locomotion. Have you noticed that Dory's friends come in many shapes and sizes? From Hank to Mr. Ray, each animal has its own way of getting where it's going!

LOCOMOTION

USE YOUR FINS!

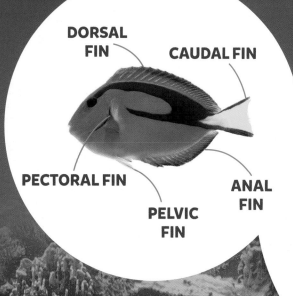

DORSAL FIN

CAUDAL FIN

PECTORAL FIN

PELVIC FIN

ANAL FIN

Fish like Dory use their fins to swim. Blue tangs have five sets of fins. Their dorsal, pelvic, and anal fins (on their backs and bellies) help them keep their balance in the water. Their caudal fins—on their tails—wave side to side and move them forward. And their pectoral fins—on their sides— help them make turns!

JET PROPULSION

Octopuses like Hank swim through the water headfirst. They take water in through their heads and squirt it out behind them. This pushes them forward really fast! But what about all those arms? Octopuses can also use them to crawl across the ocean floor.

WAVE IT AROUND

Rays swim by moving their whole bodies like a wave. Some of them also flap their sides (pectoral fins) like wings. This makes them look as if they are flying! One kind of ray, the roughtail stingray, can move really fast—up to 30 miles (48 km) per hour!

The ocean may be a dangerous place for some. Animals must stay safe to survive in the ocean. Let's look at a few ways Dory and her friends stay safe!

SURVIVAL IN THE OCEAN: STAYING SAFE

CAN'T REACH ME!

Blue tangs hide in small holes and cracks in coral reefs. When they're hiding, bigger fish like the yellowfin tuna or the tiger grouper can't reach them. Sometimes being small is a good thing! Many small fish live in coral reefs because there are so many good places to hide.

CAN'T CATCH ME!

Another way that small fish stay safe is by being fast! Sometimes the best defense is to swim away from danger. The bluelined wrasse fish is one of Dory's colorful neighbors on the coral reef. Even though they are tiny, they are some of the fastest fish in the ocean!

SAFETY IN NUMBERS

Many fish swim in large groups called schools. It's much safer swimming in a large group. Instead of seeing a tiny fish alone, hungry predators see a big mass moving through the water.

CAN'T SEE ME!

Many rays live on the ocean floor. They are amazing at hiding. Rays have different colored skin depending on where they live. This is so they can blend in with their surroundings. Some rays bury themselves under the sand to hide. When rays lie quietly in the sand, they can be almost impossible to spot! This lets them stay hidden from predators—and from prey!

Some of the same ways that ocean animals stay safe can also help them find food! Stingrays hide from both predators and prey. Schools of fish work together to stay safe and catch food. Let's learn about some of the special ways animals find and eat food!

SURVIVAL IN THE OCEAN: FINDING FOOD

FILTER FEEDERS

Big fish don't always eat big food. Just look at whale sharks! They are filter feeders. Whale sharks swim with their mouths open, sucking in lots of water filled with plankton, tiny fish, and krill. Then they filter the water through their gills and eat whatever is left!

ELECTRIC HUNTERS

Some rays eat other animals that live on the ocean floor. They have strong jaws that can crush the shells of their prey. They don't use their eyes to find food. Instead, they use electricity! A ray has sensors near its mouth that can sense the electric charge of what it's hunting. Stingrays don't hunt with their stinging tail. Their tail helps protect them from predators.

SEA ANEMONES

The sea anemone may be pretty . . . but it's also dangerous for other small animals! Many think sea anemones look like flowers, but they are really animals. They spend their whole lives attached to something hard. Their tentacles have poison darts on them. They wave their tentacles around, waiting for a fish to swim too close. When a fish gets close, the sea anemone shoots out a poison dart from its tentacles, stunning the fish, and then it pulls the fish into its mouth.

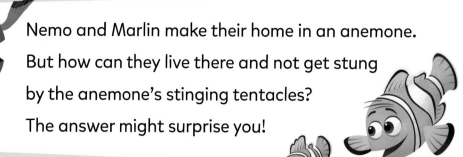

Nemo and Marlin make their home in an anemone. But how can they live there and not get stung by the anemone's stinging tentacles? The answer might surprise you!

MEET THE CLOWN FISH AND THE BLUE TANG

CLOWN FISH

Clown fish are covered in a kind of slime that protects them from the sea anemone. There are only a few fish that are safe from the poison darts in an anemone's tentacles! Clown fish make their homes in anemone tentacles. The tentacles keep clown fish safe from predators.

HELP ME HELP YOU

Sea anemones catch their own food. The clown fish living between the tentacles eat the anemone's leftovers! Clown fish help sea anemones too! They do a wiggle dance by flapping their fins and swimming in circles. All that wiggling brings fresh water into the sea anemone. This helps the anemone grow big and strong!

BACK OFF, I'M A SURGEONFISH

Blue tangs like Dory come from a family of fish called surgeonfish. They get their name because they all have at least one sharp blade next to their tail. The blade is like a surgeon's knife! Blue tangs hide from predators in cracks in the coral. But they can also use their sharp blades to protect themselves when they are threatened.

Dory's friend Hank is a master of disguise. He is so good at hiding! Octopuses have many ways to stay safe. Let's learn more about octopuses.

MEET THE OCTOPUS

COLOR AND CAMOUFLAGE

Octopuses have tiny cells under their skin that can change color. They can make their skin match their surroundings. When they do this, they are impossible to see. Octopuses are so good at this that they can even make their skin look bumpy or spiky. This way they match the rocks or coral they are lying on. Octopuses are some of the best hiders in the whole ocean!

HEY! NO GRABBING!

If a predator grabs an octopus's arm—the octopus can break off that arm and swim away. Later, once it's safe, the octopus will grow a new one. Good as new!

DON'T GET INKED!

One of the most amazing ways octopuses defend themselves is by squirting ink. Octopuses can release a cloud of dark ink to confuse their predators. While the predator is covered in ink, the octopus swims away . . . fast! The ink makes it hard to see. It also confuses a predator's sense of smell. Now that's how you hide!

Now you know that the ocean can be a scary place to live! We've seen a few examples of how Dory and her friends find food, stay warm, get oxygen, and stay safe. These are all ways that animals stay alive. Let's look at a few more ways animals can camouflage themselves in their environment.

CAMOUFLAGE

HIDING IN PLAIN SIGHT

Octopuses, stingrays, and cuttlefish are really good at blending in. They can be hard for predators or prey to see. But there's another way to stay safe, and that's to make sure you stick out! Some colors in the ocean mean danger. If an octopus suddenly starts flashing bright blue spots, it sends a message: stay away!

SHAPE-SHIFTER

SEA SNAKE

Octopuses can change shape. They can squeeze into tiny hiding spots. The best shape-shifter is the mimic octopus. It tricks predators by mimicking a different animal—from a snake to a flatfish! It does this by changing shape and also changing color. It even changes the way it moves. It can pretend to be more than fifteen other animals!

MIMIC OCTOPUS

CUTTLEFISH
CAMOUFLAGE

Cuttlefish are also great at hiding. They can change color superfast! During the day, cuttlefish are bright and colorful. At night, everything changes. They can blend into the background in the blink of an eye. They can even change the texture of their skin!

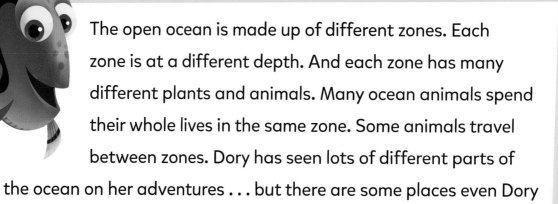

The open ocean is made up of different zones. Each zone is at a different depth. And each zone has many different plants and animals. Many ocean animals spend their whole lives in the same zone. Some animals travel between zones. Dory has seen lots of different parts of the ocean on her adventures . . . but there are some places even Dory hasn't been! Let's explore.

OPEN OCEAN

OCEAN ZONES

SUNLIGHT ZONE
SEA LEVEL

SEA TURTLE

TWILIGHT ZONE
600 FEET (180 m)

SWORDFISH

MIDNIGHT ZONE
3,000 FEET (900 m)

ANGLERFISH

SWIMMING IN THE SUNLIGHT ZONE

Whale sharks like Destiny spend most of their time near the surface. This is the sunlight zone. Other animals that live in the sunlight zone are sea turtles, jellyfish, and seals. Whale sharks and their fishy friends travel far and wide. But there's a whole world deep underneath them that they never get to see!

ENTERING THE TWILIGHT ZONE

The deeper down we go, the darker it gets. That's because the light from the sun can't travel through all that ocean water. Once we get to 600 feet (180 m) below the ocean's surface, we enter the twilight zone. It's a lot colder in the twilight zone. There is no seaweed down here. Seaweed need sunlight! Squid, hatchetfish, and jellyfish live in the twilight zone.

DEEP IN THE MIDNIGHT ZONE

Once we get down to around 3,000 feet (900 m), we enter the midnight zone. Only very special animals live down here. It is freezing cold and pitch-black. The midnight zone is home to deep-sea worms and crabs. It is also home to a very interesting animal called the anglerfish. This funny-looking fish can make a small light above its head. It waves the light around to attract other fish to eat. Making light comes in handy in the midnight zone!

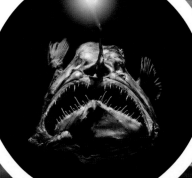

A lot of Dory's friends live close to the shore. Coastal waters are only a small part of the whole ocean. But more animals live in coastal waters than in the open ocean! The water near the coast tends to be warmer and shallower. Let's learn more about this habitat.

COASTAL WATERS

THE INTERTIDAL ZONE

Remember how we learned about the different zones of the open ocean? Well, coastal waters have zones too. There is a very busy place called the intertidal zone. The intertidal zone is where the land and the ocean meet! The sun's and the moon's gravity pull the ocean's water up and down the shore. The water is always moving. Snails, crabs, and mussels live in the intertidal zone.

SPRAY ZONE

SNAIL

HIGH TIDE ZONE

BARNACLES   SNAIL

MIDDLE TIDE ZONE

MUSSELS   CRAB

LOW TIDE ZONE

SEA STAR   KELP

SEA URCHIN

SEA OTTERS

Sea otters are amphibious mammals, just like our friends Fluke and Rudder. That means they can live on both land and water. No wonder otters live in coastal waters! They breathe air just like sea lions. They can hold their breath for a few minutes when they dive for food. Sea otters don't have any blubber. Instead, they keep warm with the thickest fur of any animal in the world! Sea otters sleep floating on their backs.

SEA STARS

Sea stars can often be found in the intertidal zone. Sometimes sea stars are also called starfish, but they are not fish. They belong to a family of animals named echinoderms, or spiny-skinned animals. That family also includes sea cucumbers, sea urchins, and sand dollars. Sea stars live on the seafloor. They move very slowly, holding on in the strong surf with many tiny suction-cupped tube feet. Sea stars can regrow an arm if they lose one!

Let's learn more about the place Dory and Nemo call home: the coral reef! Coral is a tiny animal that lives its whole life in one place. Coral is a relative of the sea anemone. Coral reefs are like giant coral cities.

CORAL REEFS

CORAL IS COLORFUL

Coral reefs are found in the warmest ocean waters. They are busy places full of plant and animal life. They are also some of the most colorful places on Earth! The water in coral reefs is the clearest in the ocean. Water here is shallow and full of sunlight. Most animals that live on coral reefs have good eyesight. All those colors tell them what they might need to stay away from!

ANCIENT ALGAE

Algae are among the oldest living things on the planet! Algae are like sea plants. They cover coral reefs. There are many kinds of algae. Algae get their energy from the sun and make oxygen. Much of the oxygen on our entire planet was made by algae. Blue tangs like Dory eat algae. This is good for the coral reefs, because it keeps the algae from growing too fast and hurting the coral.

THE GREAT BARRIER REEF

The Great Barrier Reef is the largest coral reef in the world. It is off the coast of Australia. At 1,600 miles (2,600 km) long, it is the biggest living structure on Earth. It's so big you can see it from space. It's home to fish like blue tang and clown fish. Sea turtles, stingrays, sea horses, and hundreds of other animals also live there!

Another amazing ocean habitat is the kelp forest. These forests are made up of kelp, which is a kind of algae. They are just like forests on land, except with kelp instead of trees. Kelp forests grow in much colder water than coral reefs. Let's learn more about kelp forests!

KELP FORESTS

GROWTH SPURT!

Unlike coral, which grows very slowly, kelp is one of the fastest-growing life-forms on the planet! Giant kelp can grow up to 2 feet (0.6 m) in a single day! Kelp forests often grow in rough and choppy water. This is actually good for the kelp! The water is constantly moving. This keeps the water full of fresh nutrients that help keep the kelp fed and healthy. But if the surf is too rough, it might rip the kelp off the rocks.

SAFETY FIRST

Many animals rely on kelp forests for shelter. Just like coral reefs, the forests make great places to hide. Kelp forests can also protect animals from big storms! The thick kelp forests break up the energy from the huge waves. This keeps the ocean water from getting too rough for the animals.

OTTERS AND URCHINS

Many sea urchins live in kelp forests. Sea urchins are close relatives of the sea star! They also eat a lot of kelp. If there are too many sea urchins in a kelp forest, they will eat too much kelp and kill the forest! That's where sea otters come in. Many sea otters also live in kelp forests. And otters eat a lot of urchins! Otters help the kelp survive by keeping the sea urchin population under control.

We've learned about some of the ocean's many habitats. We've explored the dark, cold midnight zone. We've been to the sunny, warm coral reefs. These places are very important for the animals that live there. But the animals are important too! Let's learn more about how Dory and her friends are important to their habitats.

EVERYONE
PLAYS A PART

ECOSYSTEMS

An ecosystem includes all the plants and animals that live there. A habitat is the place where the animals and plants live. Each part of the ecosystem relies on the other parts to survive! We've seen a few examples of ecosystems. Blue tangs like Dory use coral reefs to find food and shelter. The coral reef helps the blue tang. The blue tang eats algae. This helps keep the coral healthy. That's a perfect example of a balanced ecosystem!

THE FOOD WEB

SEA OTTERS

LARGE FISH AND OCTOPUSES

SEA URCHINS

SEA STARS

LARGER CRABS

SMALL FISH

KELP

PLANKTON

A food web is a map of all the different plants and animals and what they eat. Each ecosystem has its own food web. Remember the sea otters and the sea urchins in the kelp forest? They are both part of the kelp forest's food web. Every single animal and plant in a habitat plays its part. Sometimes they eat food, and sometimes they are food!

PEOPLE AND THE OCEAN

People are part of the giant ecosystem that is the planet Earth! The ocean is very important to our survival. We are important to the ocean too. It is up to us to help keep this ecosystem balanced. We can do this by protecting ocean animals from overfishing and pollution.

DORY'S OCEAN HOME

Dory's coral reef is a magical place. It is just one of the habitats in the ocean. Each habitat is part of an ecosystem. The plants and animals in a place help keep it healthy and growing. We are all a part of the amazing balance of life on this planet.

CHAPTER 3

The Science of Cars

WHAT IS A CAR?

Lightning McQueen's friends come in many different shapes and sizes. They are all marvelous machines that use their own power to get from one place to another—or quickly around a racetrack. Let's take a peek under the hood and explore the amazing machines we call cars.

It's a Big Group!

Cars are part of the big group of vehicles called automobiles, or motorized vehicles. In that group, you will find cars, trucks, buses, and vans. You will even find tractors, bulldozers, and fire trucks. There are different kinds of vehicles for different kinds of jobs.

What Every Vehicle Needs

Every vehicle has an engine. The engine uses some kind of fuel for energy. A gasoline engine converts gasoline, or gas, into motion to get a car moving. An engine in an electric vehicle is called a motor. An electric car delivers power from the batteries to the motor.

Let's Get Rolling!

Fuel runs the engine or motor, which sends power to the wheels. That power makes the wheels move. Let's find out more about how these great machines work.

CARS TO RACE AND RIDE

Sterling owns the Rust-eze Racing Center. Cars train there to become better racers. But what exactly makes a car a race car? What does a race car have that a family car or commuter car doesn't?

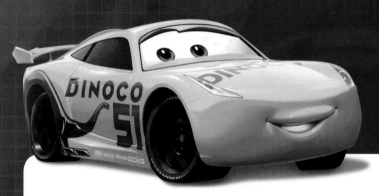

Fast Cars

A race car like Cruz Ramirez is built for speed! Her body, engine, and tires help her go as fast as she safely can on the racetrack.

Family Cars

A family car or a minivan is not for racing. Its job is to carry you and your friends or family on the road—not on the racetrack. It is built to keep you safe and comfortable.

Commuter Cars

Any car, except a race car, can be a commuter car. Its main job is to travel from home to work and back every day. Many of the best commuter cars are small, comfortable, and safe.

ALL SYSTEMS GO!

Smokey was the Fabulous Hudson Hornet's crew chief. If a car is in trouble, he can find the trouble and fix it! Smokey understands that a car is made up of many different systems. All the systems have to work together to keep a car running.

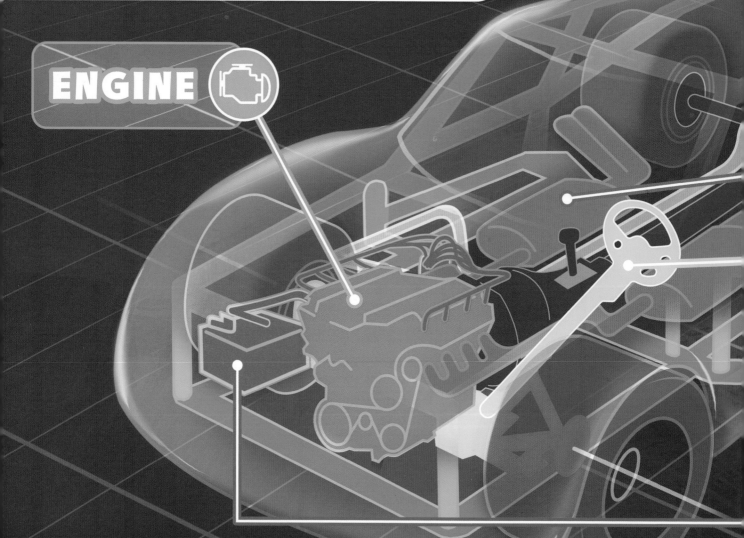

ENGINE

FUEL SYSTEM

 DRIVETRAIN

TIRES & BRAKES

 EXHAUST

 STEERING

 BODY & CHASSIS

 ELECTRICAL SYSTEM

MAKING THE METAL MOVE

Doc was Lightning's crew chief. Doc knew that every car starts with several main systems—the engine, the drivetrain, the chassis, the steering, and the brakes.

The Engine

A car without an engine will not move. The engine is the thing that all the other systems count on. The engine provides the power to all the systems in the car.

The Drivetrain

The engine's main job is to burn fuel and turn it into energy. That energy is transferred to the drivetrain, which is connected to the back or sometimes the side of the engine. The drivetrain delivers the power produced in the engine to the wheels so the car can move. The gears in the transmission help control how fast or slow the car goes.

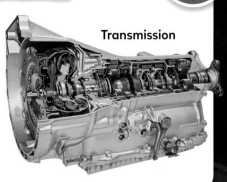

Transmission

The Body and the Chassis

A chassis is the supporting frame of the car. A car's engine, tires, and other mechanical parts are bolted to the chassis.

The body of a car is made up of large panels. The body is designed to protect a car's riders. A car's engine, transmission, and other systems can sometimes be found within the body.

Chassis with wheels and tires

Unibody design with wheels and tires

In many race cars, trucks, and older cars like Doc or Smokey, the chassis and the body are made as two separate pieces and then fastened together. But most cars made today have a unibody design. The frame and the basic body shell are made together. A chassis and body that are made as one big piece is easier and faster to build. A car with a unibody design is also lighter, quieter, and safer.

FUEL THE MACHINE

Before leaving the Cotter Pin, River Scott stops to fill up at the gasoline pump outside the door. Why? Because gas keeps a car's engine running! Gas is the fuel still used by most cars today—but that is changing.

Explosive Power

Cutaway of an internal combustion engine

fuel tank

fuel pump

fuel line

engine

An engine that uses gas has a special name. It is called an internal combustion engine. *Internal* means "inside." *Combustion* means "burning." Fuel is pumped into the engine where—at just the right time—a tiny electrical spark sets off an explosion. The force of that explosion is the power that makes the wheels move.

Reducing Pollution

The fuel internal combustion engines burn is not good for our air. More and more cars are being manufactured without internal combustion engines. Their engines use electricity for fuel, not gas. Instead of stopping to fill the car's gas tank, a driver stops to recharge the car's big batteries.

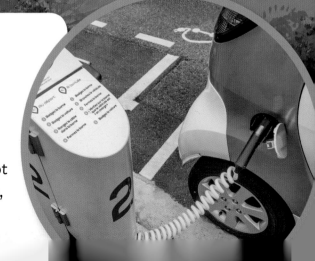

Get Comfortable

Electricity can help a car run. You can also thank electricity for a lot of things that keep you comfortable inside a car. The radio, lights, heater, windows, and sometimes even the seats all use electricity.

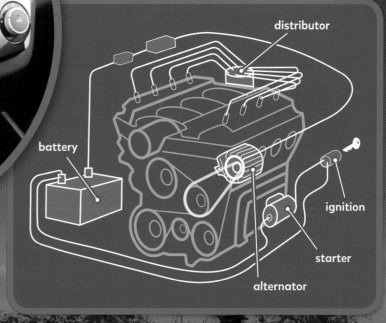

distributor

battery

ignition

starter

alternator

THROTTLE UP!

Cruz Ramirez is a fast racer. She knows that the engine is the power center of a car. Most engines use gasoline for fuel, but they also need electricity. Spark plugs deliver the electricity needed to ignite the fuel inside the engine. This creates the energy needed to make the car move.

Inside a Gas Engine

Inside a car's engine, there are one or two rows of closed, sealed tubes called cylinders. Tiny explosions inside the cylinders make energy that becomes the force that moves the car. There are thousands of these explosions every minute! Most passenger cars have four cylinders. But bigger cars, trucks, and race cars could have six, eight, ten, and even twelve cylinders. The more cylinders an engine has, the more power the engine can usually make.

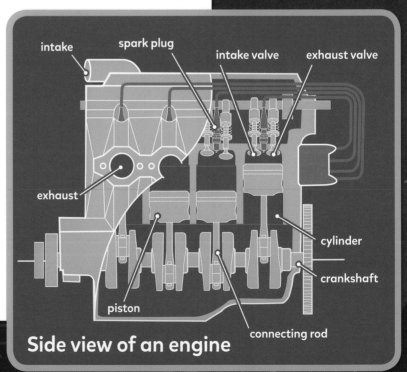

intake   spark plug   intake valve   exhaust valve

exhaust

cylinder

crankshaft

piston

connecting rod

Side view of an engine

It's Explosive

Let's take a look inside a four-cylinder engine and see where and how these explosions happen. Each cylinder goes through four steps, called strokes.

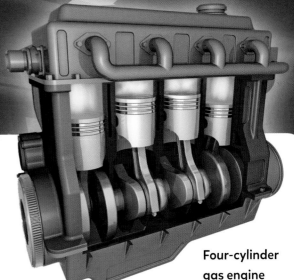

Four-cylinder gas engine

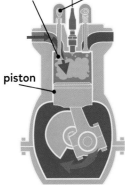

Front view of cylinder

Stroke 1: Intake

During the intake stroke, the piston moves down from the top of the cylinder. The camshaft opens the intake valve. A few drops of gas enter the cylinder, and the intake valve closes tight.

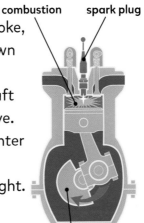

Stroke 3: Combustion

The distributor sends electricity through a wire to the spark plug. The tiny spark makes the air and gas mixture ignite and expand. This explosion pushes the piston back down. That force turns the crankshaft to make the wheels move.

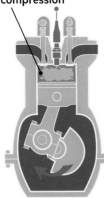

Stroke 2: Compression

The piston is pushed back up and squeezes the air and gas tightly together. This compression makes the explosion more powerful.

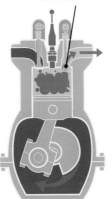

Stroke 4: Exhaust

During the exhaust stroke, the piston moves back up and the camshaft opens the exhaust valve. The piston pushes the burned fuel out of the cylinder through the open exhaust valve and into the car's exhaust system.

One cylinder by itself would not have the power to move a modern car. But most car engines have at least four cylinders working together at the same time—and they make a superpowerful team!

GET INTO GEAR

The crankshaft in a car's engine rotates thousands of times every minute! It is connected to the transmission, which controls the amount of power going from the engine to the wheels. The transmission keeps the engine from working too hard. It also makes sure that the wheels get the power they need for the speed the driver wants. Experienced racers like Jackson Storm and Lightning McQueen know the art of choosing the right gear at the right time to stay in the race.

Lots of Gears!

The transmission attaches to the engine. There are lots of gears in the transmission. The gears work together to transfer the engine's power to the wheels.

engine

transmission

differential

clutch

driveshaft

wheel

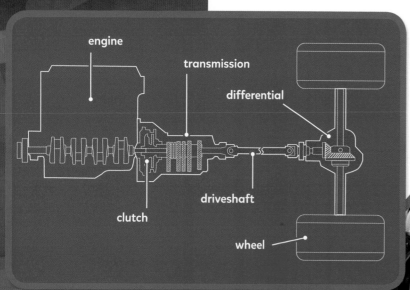

Manual Transmission

There are two main kinds of car transmissions. One is manual transmission, and the other is automatic transmission.

With a manual transmission, the driver decides when to shift the gears for the best power. It takes skill and practice. The driver takes one foot off the gas and steps on the clutch pedal with the other foot. This disconnects the engine from the transmission. The driver then moves the gear selector into gear, takes his or her foot off the clutch pedal, and steps on the gas again.

Gear selector for manual transmission

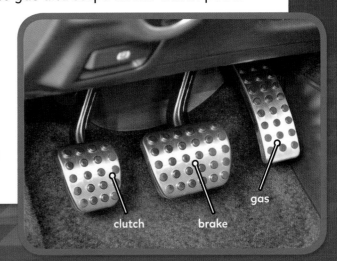

clutch   brake   gas

Automatic Transmission

Cars with automatic transmissions do all the shifting themselves. To get the car into gear, the driver moves the gearshift to either D for drive or R for reverse. The transmission does the rest! The transmission uses the best gear for the engine, while the driver concentrates on the road. There is no clutch pedal in a car with automatic transmission. The driver has a gas pedal and a brake pedal.

Gearshift for automatic transmission

PUSH ME, PULL ME

Racing legend Louise "Barnstormer" Nash has a rear-wheel drive (RWD) system. But what exactly does that mean? What is the difference between rear-wheel drive, front-wheel drive (FWD), four-wheel drive (4WD), and all-wheel drive (AWD)? It's good to know what kind of drive system a car has, because that tells which wheels actually get the power to make the car move.

Rear-wheel drive system

Rear-Wheel Drive

Most older cars, trucks, buses, and some sports cars on the road today have a rear-wheel drive system. This means that the power moves from the engine through the transmission to the rear or back wheels of the car. The rear wheels push the car forward. Most race car drivers prefer rear-wheel drive. They believe it helps the car perform better when swinging through tight curves on the track. The car has better balance with the heavy engine in front and the push from the back.

Front-Wheel Drive

Front-wheel drive system

Many passenger cars built today have front-wheel drive, where the engine's power is delivered to the front wheels. With power coming from the front wheels, the car is pulled instead of pushed. Drivers of family cars and commuter cars feel they are easier to drive. With the heavy engine adding to the weight in front, many drivers feel this system gives better traction on hills and in snow. Front-wheel drive is also safer for turning.

Using All the Wheels

An all-wheel drive system can change which axle has the power. If the car senses the wheels on one axle are slipping, it will send power to the other axle to get better traction. This can help keep a car moving over mud, wet roads, snow, ice, or sand. All-wheel drive systems are found in many newer family vehicles and SUVs.

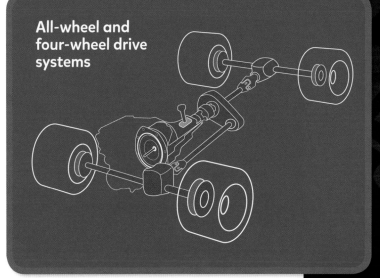

All-wheel and four-wheel drive systems

A four-wheel drive vehicle delivers the engine's power to all four wheels at the same time. Having this control can be great for driving where there are no roads at all—like up a steep dirt hill, over rocks, or through a stream! Each of the wheels gets power for maximum traction.

HIT THE BRAKES

Ka-chow! Lightning knows how to zip around superfast on a racetrack. But he also knows that being able to *stop* is just as important as being able to *go*. It's all about the brakes!

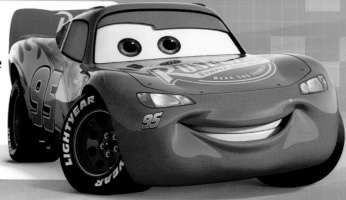

Drum Brakes

Legends like River Scott and Junior Moon have drum brakes. Racers like Lightning McQueen, Jackson Storm, and most modern vehicles on the road today use disc brakes. Both brake systems will stop a car, but disc brakes do it better.

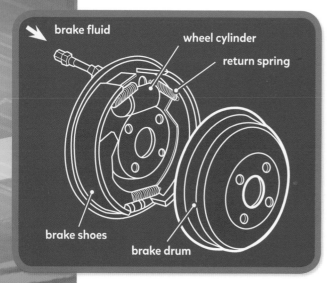

brake fluid

wheel cylinder

return spring

brake shoes

brake drum

The drum in a drum brake system is made out of heavy steel. When a driver with drum brakes steps on the brake pedal, it pushes two curved brake shoes against the inside of the spinning drum. This causes heat and friction. The friction slows down the wheel. You can't see the brake shoes in a drum brake system because they are covered by the drum.

Disc Brakes

Disc brakes have a clamp called a caliper. Brake pads inside the caliper squeeze both sides of the disc at the same time. This slows down the wheels and the car. The disc can be made out of iron, but many—especially those on race cars—are made from lighter carbon composite material or ceramic.

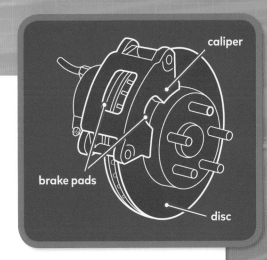

caliper

brake pads

disc

Most drivers like disc brakes better than drum brakes. Disc brakes are stronger and last a long time. They cool down faster because they are open to the air. Drum brakes are covered up and can't cool down as fast. They can get too hot to work and usually wear out sooner.

Extra Help for Slippery Roads

Good racers know many tricks to keep from losing control of their cars. Most cars made today have an extra helper with their brakes—the antilock braking system, or ABS.

Sensors on every wheel measure its speed. Special pumps and a computer can tell when a tire starts to skid on a wet road. When that happens, the ABS takes control of the brakes on all four wheels. It does everything it can to keep those wheels from skidding. It works to get the car going straight again. ABS is like having an experienced race car driver take over until the danger is past!

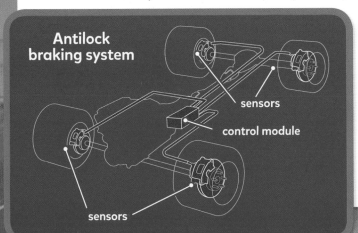

Antilock braking system

sensors

control module

sensors

KEEP THE RUBBER ON THE ROAD

There are different tires for different track surfaces. Whether the track is wet or dry, made of asphalt or dirt, Luigi and Guido know the right tire can make the winning difference!

Tires for a Dry Track

Racers are happiest when the track is dry and the weather is mild. On dry days, race cars use special tires called slicks. They got that name because they have no treads. They are completely slick!

Slicks Need to Stick!

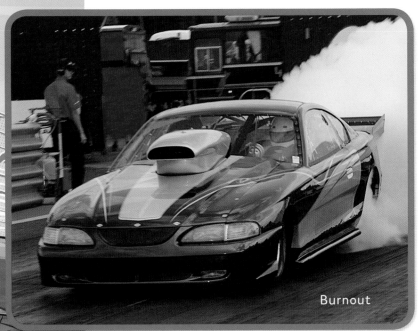

Burnout

Many racers on today's racetracks might take warm-up laps before the flag drops. They will slowly swerve back and forth. They are not practicing steering. They are "scrubbing" their front tires to get them warm and soft so that they will stick to the asphalt on fast turns.

In a drag race, where there are no turns, cars need their *back* tires to stick. Drag racers might force only the back tires to spin superfast to make them hot. This is called a burnout. Hot tires stick better to the track.

Watch the Weather!

The race officials keep a careful eye on the weather during a long race. If it looks like rain, it may be time for a tire change. Those slicks will not work at all on a wet track. It's time to make a quick pit stop and change to "wets." The tread on these tires will help throw the water to the side to keep the car sticking to the track on those slippery laps.

Racing tires don't last very long. A good tire on a passenger car can be safe for thousands of miles of driving. But race car tires, often driving at over 150 miles (241 km) per hour, may need to be changed several times during a single race.

SAFETY FIRST

Sheriff enforces traffic and driving laws to make sure the roads are safe for everyone. Good drivers think about safety all the time. Let's look at some of the things that make cars safe.

Beep-Beep!

One of the first safety features added to cars was the horn. Making a loud noise is a good way to get other drivers to pay attention and stay alert. However, the loud blast from a horn can be shocking. A driver should never use it without a good reason.

Belts and Bags

When a car is racing forward and suddenly crashes into something, it stops. But everything *inside* the car keeps going. Books, cups, and sandwiches go flying through the air. So can the driver and passengers. That's why all modern cars have seat belts and airbags. Seat belts hold passengers safely in their seats. Everyone in the car should wear them. An airbag provides extra protection in a crash. In less than a second, a big pillow pops out from inside the car and quickly fills up with air to cushion the driver and any passengers.

The Crumple Zone

The car is crunched, but you are not! Most modern cars have crumple zones in the front and back. Crumple zones soften a crash to protect passengers. The crumple zones are designed to absorb energy in a crash. This keeps the full force of the crash away from the driver and any passengers.

There might be a terrible accident at the racetrack. A car rolls and turns and hits a wall. Parts are flying in all directions. But when the dust clears, the driver stands up and waves to the crowd! The car has completely fallen apart. But it was made to break away from the driver, who was protected in the safety zone.

crumple zone   safety zone   crumple zone

Crash test dummy

Safety Testing

Carmakers constantly come up with new ideas to keep people safe in a crash. Those ideas and designs are tested using life-size models of people. These models are crash test dummies. They are built to look and move like humans. Crash test dummies have special sensors that send important information to the carmakers about what happens in a crash. That information tells the designers what needs to change to make the car safer for people in an accident.

NO DRAG, PLEASE!

Next-gen racers like Jackson Storm think a lot about speed and efficiency. They will do everything they can to reduce drag. *Drag* is exactly what it sounds like—"something that slows you down." The biggest cause of drag is air. Race car manufacturers have a few tricks to make cars more aerodynamic. They want air to work with the car instead of slowing it down.

Wings

A wing on a sports car

Air is always rushing over, under, and around a moving car. This creates drag and makes the car work harder to move forward. At the super-high speeds on a racetrack, that air can actually lift the back wheels off the ground. A wing, or airfoil, looks like a small, upside-down airplane wing. It is mounted across the back of a race car. The wing pushes the air *up* and forces the back end of the car *down*. This is called downforce. Downforce pushes the rear tires of a Formula One race car onto the track. The car can speed through a turn faster without spinning out of control.

Spoilers

Piston Cup race cars like Cal Weathers have the same trouble with air as Formula One race cars. But instead of wings, they use spoilers to force the airflow around and *away* from the car. The spoiler attaches to the back of the car and forces the air to stream over the top of the car. Without the spoiler, the air could lift the tail end of the car. A rear spoiler reduces drag and helps keep those back tires sticking to the road.

There is such a thing as too much downforce, though. Too much downforce creates drag. So racers always experiment with the angle of their spoilers and wings. They try to find just the right balance between downforce and drag.

A spoiler on a sports car

A sports car with a carbon fiber finish panel

Weight

How much a car weighs can have a big effect on drag, speed, handling, and fuel efficiency. The material that cars are made of has changed over the years. Car frames and bodies used to be made mostly of steel. Steel is strong, but it is also very heavy. Weight creates drag. Drag reduces speed and makes the engine burn more fuel.

Race car designers thought cars could get faster by losing some weight. They began mixing aluminum into vehicle bodies. Aluminum is strong like steel but is much lighter.

Some steel and aluminum parts in commuter and race cars are now being replaced with an even lighter material called carbon fiber. Carbon fiber is a kind of cloth that can be woven together and piled into layers. Then it is covered with special hard glue called epoxy. Car parts made with carbon fiber are stronger than steel and much lighter. A car made with carbon fiber has less weight to push around the track.

GET in LINE

New cars are built on an assembly line at a factory. Lizzie knows all about the assembly line. She is a Ford Model T. The Model T was the first car to be produced on an assembly line. On an assembly line, engines are put together and bodies are formed. Electric wires are connected, and drivetrains are attached. Doors are put in place. Windshields, seats, wheels, and brakes are installed. The modern automobile factory does everything that goes into making a car.

One Step at a Time

Almost every car in the world today came from a factory assembly line. It is called a line because the cars move down in a line to the workers. The workers usually stay in one place. When a car reaches a worker, the worker does the same job on each car.

Cars move down the assembly line to the workers.

Robots Work Hard!

Robots do a lot of work at factories. They are fast and strong. They can do some of the hardest and most dangerous jobs. Robots often build the chassis and car bodies. You will also find robots doing most of the painting. They work in spots that humans cannot reach.

Robots on the assembly line

Paints for Color and Protection

Ramone is an artist. He knows more than any other car about paint and decoration. Some factories use five different kinds of paint to protect a car. One special coat of paint keeps rust away. Another layer of paint protects the car from the sun. The bottom of the car gets painted with an undercoating. This keeps dirt from sticking to the bottom of the car. The undercoating also blocks any water from getting between the frame and the body. The busy team of robots in the painting rooms can spend hours finishing just one car. At the end of a day, humans and robots sharing the work on an assembly line can finish hundreds of cars.

Robots on the painting line

Cars at the end of the assembly line are ready for inspection.

AMAZING CAR CULTURES

Ramone likes to cruise low 'n' slow, sporting his latest paint job. All around the world, many car owners belong to different car cultures. They have a lot of fun making their cars look different and special. They like to get together and show off their hard work.

Lowriders

Have you ever seen a car hopping up and down while slowly driving down the street? Then you have probably seen a lowrider like Ramone. The bodies of these cars are very, very low to the ground, but they have special shock absorbers that can push and pump the wheels up and down whenever the driver wants.

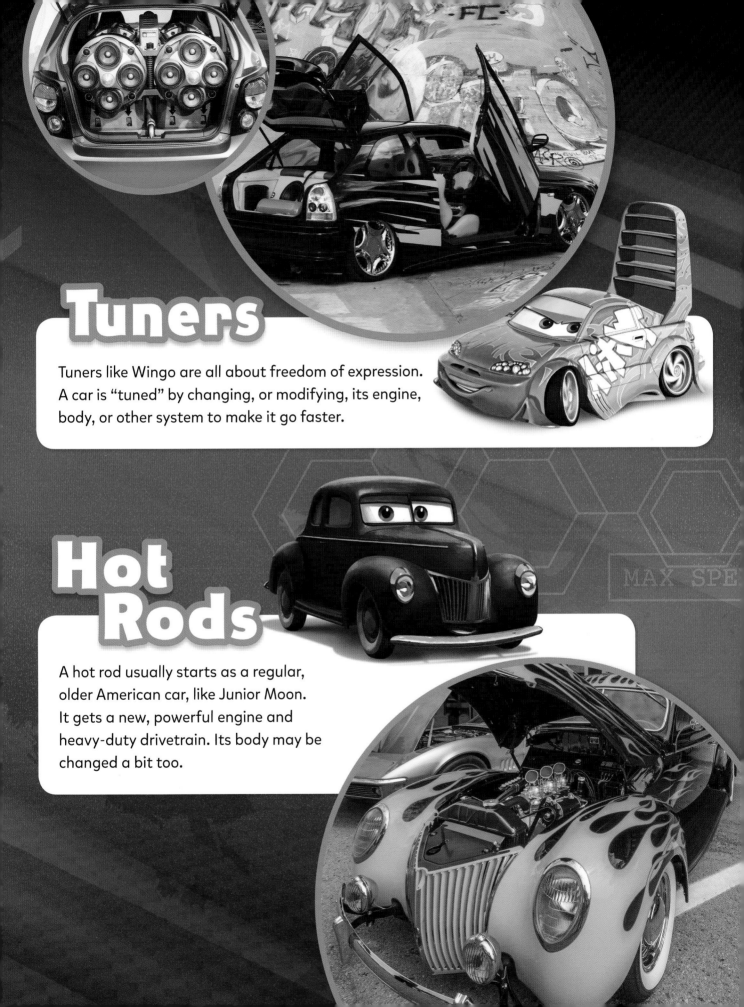

Tuners

Tuners like Wingo are all about freedom of expression. A car is "tuned" by changing, or modifying, its engine, body, or other system to make it go faster.

Hot Rods

A hot rod usually starts as a regular, older American car, like Junior Moon. It gets a new, powerful engine and heavy-duty drivetrain. Its body may be changed a bit too.

START YOUR ENGINES!

Next-gen racers like Bubba Wheelhouse are built for speed. Race cars today are a blend of technology and smart design. Let's take a look at different kinds of race cars, the tracks they run on, and the races they compete in.

Two Kinds of Race Cars

Race cars can be divided into two main types. There are open-wheel cars and closed-wheel cars. It is easy to tell the difference. A closed-wheel car is one where the wheels are covered by the car's body or fender. Stock cars and cars that race on rally circuits feature a closed-wheel design. The wheels on an open-wheel car are seen outside the car's main body. Formula One and Indy cars are good examples.

An open-wheel Indy car

A closed-wheel rally car

Stock Cars

Stock car racing got its name because at first the cars were regular assembly-line, or stock, vehicles.

Then people began making their own changes to these cars. The cars got faster and more powerful, and the races became too dangerous. An organization called NASCAR set up rules about the kinds of improvements a car can have. Today, NASCAR races are the most popular races in North America.

The Daytona 500

Stock cars racing at the Daytona 500

NASCAR races feature stock cars, like Bobby Swift. The most famous stock car race is the Daytona 500 in Daytona Beach, Florida. The Daytona 500 is 500 miles (805 km) long. About fifty cars go two hundred laps around the 2.5-mile (4 km) track. Even though these heavy cars are going 200 miles (322 km) per hour around a big oval track, it is okay for them to have contact. That is a nice way of saying that they can try to push one another out of the way!

FORMULA ONE RACING

Francesco Bernoulli is a Formula One race car. Every Formula One car is built and designed by its own team. Their secret design can change whenever they think of something that might work better. Formula One teams have the biggest budgets in the world—between $300 and $400 million! That money goes a long way in building the best car.

Built Right, Inside and Out

Designing a Formula One car isn't easy. Hard work goes into making sure that the body, wings, and spoilers provide the very best possible balance between drag, traction, and speed. When drivers are racing through the course's twisty turns, they want their tires stuck to the road. As a result, Formula One cars are a little bit slower than Indy cars— but not by much. Their top speed is still about 225 miles (360 km) per hour!

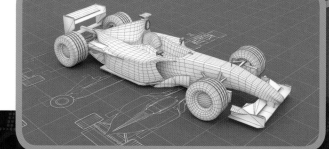

The Circuit

Formula One racers like circuits and street courses with plenty of twists, turns, and hills. Many Formula One circuits are a mix of street and track. The roads are closed to local traffic. This gives room for race cars to zoom up and down hills, around sharp turns, down narrow straightaways, and even through tunnels!

Formula One cars on the Monte Carlo circuit in Monaco

The Monaco Grand Prix

The most famous Formula One race is the Monaco Grand Prix in Europe. It takes place entirely on Monaco's city streets. The course is very narrow. It is also extremely dangerous. It is difficult for a driver to pass another car. This is one race in which a driver's skill is more important than the power of the car.

Monaco Grand Prix circuit

INDYCAR AND DRAG RACING

Jackson Storm has been clocked at an impressive 214 miles (344 km) per hour. But he wouldn't be able to keep up with the record-breaking speed of an Indy car or a top fuel dragster. An Indy car can reach a speed of 240 miles (385 km) per hour. A top fuel dragster goes almost 100 miles (160 km) per hour faster—that's an amazing 335 miles (540 km) per hour!

Indy Cars

All cars used in IndyCar racing have the exact same design. One company provides the chassis, and another provides the engine. Each car has the same body and parts. The difference lies in the driver. Because every car is the same, drivers depend on their skills at top speed on straightaways.

Most Indy cars race only in North America. Their most famous race is on the oval track of the Indianapolis 500 in Indianapolis, Indiana.

Indianapolis 500

The Indianapolis 500 is a race held once a year at the Indianapolis Motor Speedway. It is just for Indy cars. The speedway is one of the biggest racetracks in the world. It has a giant 2.5 mile (4 km) oval track and a curvy track too. Drivers make two hundred laps around the oval track. That's 500 miles (805 km) of racing!

The front straightaway at the 2015 Indianapolis 500

Drag Racing

The big lights turn green. Two cars race down a straight track for a quarter mile (0.4 km) as fast as they can! A drag race can feature all kinds of vehicles—even trucks and motorcycles. For a sports car, the whole race lasts less than fifteen seconds. If you race a top fuel dragster, you will finish by the time you count to four. It goes so fast that cars need parachutes to help them stop!

DEMOLITION DERBY, ENDURANCE, AND RALLY RACING

Raoul ÇaRoule is known as the World's Greatest Rally Car. He drives on any road surface and in all types of weather. Let's take a look at some races and events where skill, speed, and endurance are put to the test.

24 Hours of Le Mans Endurance Race

The 24 Hours of Le Mans is an endurance race that lets drivers test how well cars hold up over twenty-four hours of high-speed driving. The race takes place on a nearly 8.5-mile (14 km) circuit that includes both a curvy track and closed streets. Pit stops in this race are as important as the driving. Tires are changed, and fuel tanks are filled. Sometimes repairs are made. Drivers jump out and make way for their driving partners. It is very exciting to watch!

A pit stop during the 24 Hours of Le Mans in 2014

World Rally Championship

Rally races take the driving off the paved road and onto ice, snow, gravel, and dirt. The World Rally Championship (WRC) is made up of thirteen three-day rallies that take place throughout the year. Each rally is held in a different country and is divided into fifteen to twenty-five stages. These stages can each be up to 15 miles (24 km) long. A driver and a codriver have to complete each stage in as little time as possible. World Rally cars look a lot like cars you see on the road. But they are lighter, more powerful, and just a bit safer.

Demolition Derby

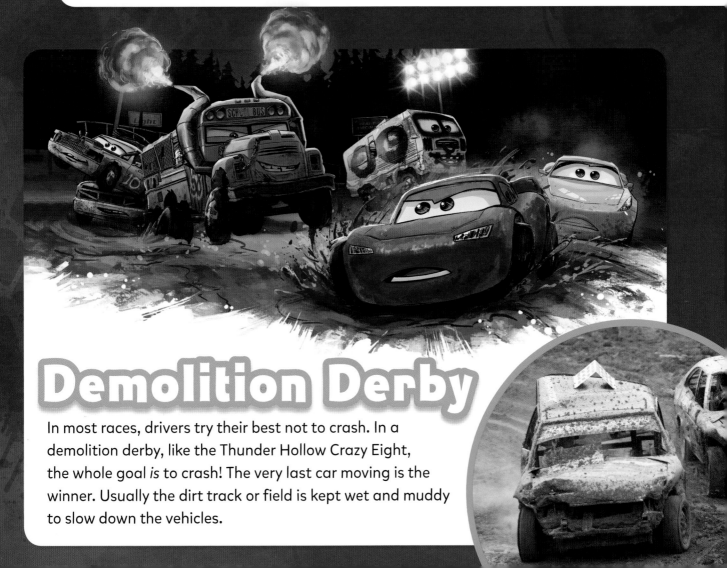

In most races, drivers try their best not to crash. In a demolition derby, like the Thunder Hollow Crazy Eight, the whole goal *is* to crash! The very last car moving is the winner. Usually the dirt track or field is kept wet and muddy to slow down the vehicles.

CARS OF THE FUTURE

Automobiles have changed quite a bit over the years—from a great legend like the Fabulous Hudson Hornet to a next-gen racer like Chase Racelott. Let's take a look at what the future might hold for everyday cars that cruise the roads.

Safer Cars

Making cars safer is an ongoing mission. Some cars now have cameras that show what's behind them. And some cars have special sensors to warn you about cars next to you. These sensors can tell if you are too close to another car. Some cars can even correct your steering or put on the brakes to avoid a crash.

Many new cars have airbags in the doors to protect you from a side-impact collision. Some carmakers are experimenting with airbags placed underneath a car to help stop a vehicle before a crash.

Driverless Cars

Would you ride in a car without a driver? Well, very soon you may have your chance! Many carmakers are testing driverless cars right now. These cars have cameras, lasers, radar, and special sensors to show them where to steer. These cars will be able to "talk" to one another so they stay out of one another's way. Soon you might be able to order a car without a driver to pick you up and take you to your destination.

Flying Cars?

Wouldn't it be fun to have a car that could lift itself into the air and fly to where you needed to go? Inventors have been imagining ways to do that for a long time.

There are a few flying cars today. But they look more like airplanes than cars. Most have long wings that unfold, and they need a runway to take off and land. The very best kind of flying car in the future might be one that can hop straight up into the air from the road. Some might have rotors like a helicopter's that unfold from the top. Others may use giant fans on the bottom of the car that push it into the air.

THE ROAD AHEAD

From old assembly line cars like Lizzie to modern racing cars like Lightning, car technology has changed a lot over the years. And the magical world of cars keeps developing. What do you think the future might hold for cars? Buckle up and rev your engines—it's sure to be an exciting ride!

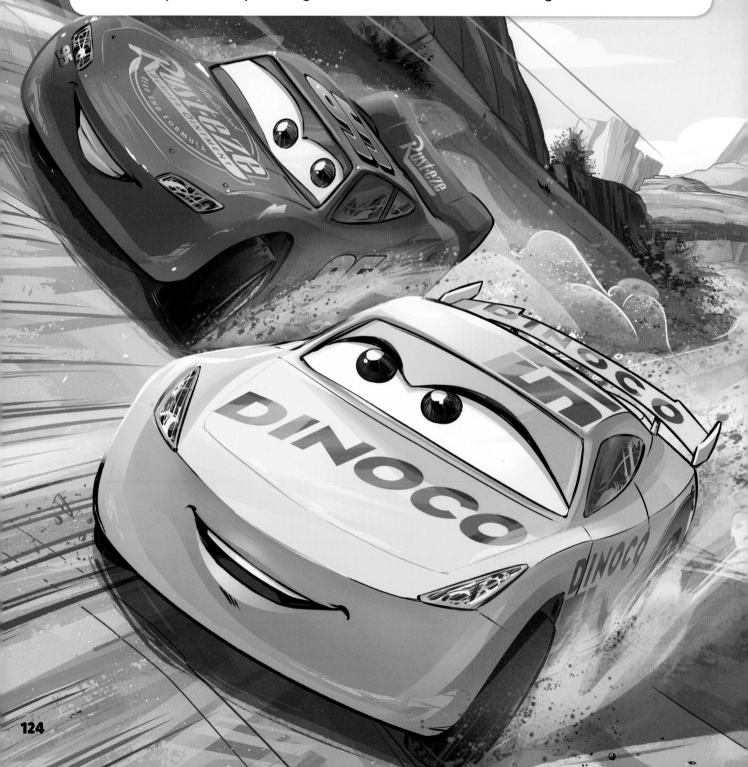

CHAPTER 4

The Pacific Islands

WELCOME TO THE PACIFIC ISLANDS!

Welcome! Let's explore the amazing place Moana and her friends call home: the Pacific Islands!

Pacific Ocean

Where in the World?

The Pacific Ocean is the largest and deepest ocean in the world. It covers more than one-third of the globe! The Pacific Islands are in the Pacific Ocean. The Pacific Islands are also known as Oceania. All kinds of plants, animals, and people call Oceania home.

Meet the Islanders

Meet Moana, her family, and her friends. Gramma Tala may have a tale or two to tell. Maui, the shape-shifter and demigod of the wind and sea, is here too. He may be a bit boastful, but he is—after all—a hero. And let's not forget Heihei, Moana's silly rooster, or her pet pig Pua. They will be your guides as you venture on your quest to learn more about the Pacific Islands.

Exploring the Islands

Let's discover some of the plants and animals of the Pacific Islands. Then we can find out what many Pacific Islanders eat and drink, what kinds of clothes they wear, and what music they might play. And of course we can't forget about wayfinding, the special way Pacific Islanders found their way from island to island.

ISLAND STORIES

Moana's grandmother Tala knows many stories. Ever since Moana was a little girl, she's listened to Gramma tell her tales. Moana has learned much about her people, her ancestors, and her island from the tales Tala tells.

Gramma Tala Tells Tales

What are Gramma Tala's stories about? They are about the island where she lives. They are about her ancestors. They are about the ways her people live and the ways they have lived. Her stories are very important to Moana, her family, and her friends.

Oral History

We don't always know the exact dates and times for events from the past in the Pacific Islands. This is because stories in the past weren't written down as they are now. Instead, they were spoken out loud. Stories were told by storytellers like Gramma Tala. These storytellers passed the stories down to their children and their children's children. This is called oral history. This kind of storytelling connects people to one another and to their past.

Many Islands, Many Stories

The Pacific Islands are rich with stories. There are many countries in the Pacific Islands. Each has its own language. While many of these languages and stories are connected, they are also different. Each island has its own culture and its own tales to tell.

THE PACIFIC ISLANDS

There are more than twenty thousand islands in the Pacific Ocean. Only some of these islands have people on them.

The Three -nesias!

The Pacific Islands are divided into three groups: Melanesia, which means "black islands"; Micronesia, which means "small islands"; and Polynesia, which means "many islands." The "nesia" part of the names come from a Greek word that means "island."

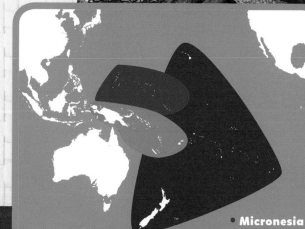

- Micronesia
- Melanesia
- Polynesia

Samoa and Tonga

Two of the countries in Polynesia are Samoa and Tonga. People have lived on those islands for more than two thousand years. Samoa means "sacred center." Tonga is made up of 171 islands! Fewer than half of the islands in Tonga have people on them.

Samoa

Tonga

Hawai'i and New Zealand

Hawai'i

New Zealand

Two of the last islands that were settled in Polynesia are Hawai'i and New Zealand. Hawai'i is in the northern part of Polynesia. New Zealand is very far south. Hawai'i is part of the United States. The first settlers traveled over 2,000 miles (3,200 km) by canoe to reach Hawai'i. Early Pacific settlers made an even longer trip to New Zealand about twelve hundred years ago. They named their home Aotearoa. This name is still used today.

FLORA OF THE ISLANDS

Moana's fictional island, Motunui, is full of plants, trees, and flowers. All the plants in a place are called the flora. There's a huge variety of flora in the Pacific Islands. Because there are so many islands, there are many different climates and types of flora.

Rain Forests

Some islands have a dry side and a wet side. On the wet side of many islands, there are mountains. And on many of these islands with mountains, there are also rain forests. Fiji, Samoa, and Tahiti all have rain forests. Because it rains so much, rain forests are home to many different plants and trees.

Grasslands

On the dry side of some islands, there are grasslands. Grasslands can often be found where there is less wind. Hawai'i and Fiji have grasslands. Grasslands are home to many kinds of grasses, but they have few trees.

So Many Plants!

Three of the most common plants in the Pacific Islands are ferns, mangroves, and coconut palms. Ferns are some of the oldest plants on Earth! They grow in forests and near the shore too. Mangroves are trees that live right next to the ocean. Unlike most trees, they can survive in salt water. Coconut palm trees have coconuts on them . . . of course! They can grow to be almost 100 feet (30 m) tall.

Ferns

Mangroves

Coconut palms

FAUNA OF THE ISLANDS

Moana's animal friends, Pua and Heihei, are part of the fauna on Moana's island home. All the animals in a place are called the fauna. Many kinds of animals live on different islands of the Pacific.

Native and Non-Native Animals

The first Pacific Islanders brought many animals with them when they explored. These are called non-native animals. Animals that are originally from a place are called native animals. Bats called flying foxes are one kind of animal native to Fiji. What about Pua and Heihei? Pigs and chickens were brought to the islands thousands of years ago.

Fijian flying foxes

Collared kingfisher

Birds

Many kinds of birds are native to the Pacific Islands. They include parrots, doves, kingfishers, herons, swallows, and warblers. Many of these birds are seabirds.

Sea Creatures

Many sea creatures live in the waters around the Pacific Islands. Sea turtles, dolphins, and whales live off the coast of Fiji. Clown fish, crabs, and tuna swim in the waters of the Marshall Islands. Manta rays, squid, and sea lions can be found by Hawai'i. The ocean is full of life.

Butterfly fish

FOOD AND DRINK

What do Pacific Islanders eat? What do they drink? Is it similar to what you eat and drink?

Fishing and Farming

Many islanders fish for food. The first Pacific Islanders got much of their food from the ocean. Even today Pacific Islanders still use canoes to fish off the coast. Islanders also grow their food. Villages farm yams, breadfruit, and taro. They also grow many kinds of fruit, including bananas, mangoes, and pineapples.

Breadfruit

Yams

Taro root

The Amazing Coconut

The coconut is one of the most important fruits in all the Pacific Islands. Islanders use every single part of the coconut. They drink the water inside the coconut. They eat the coconut's meat. They turn the meat into coconut milk and cook with it. They use the husks to make rope and string. They use the shells to make bowls.

Drinking Water

Where do Pacific Islanders get their drinking water? Not from the ocean. The water from the ocean is too salty. Many islands have fresh water lakes, waterfalls, and pools. Many islanders collect rainwater and save it. Sometimes the only fresh water on an island is found underground.

ISLAND HOUSES

What kind of houses did Pacific Islanders in Moana's time live in? Do their homes look like yours?

The *Fale*

In Tonga and Samoa, a house is called a *fale*. Early Samoans and Tongans built *fale* using only what they had on the island. Samoans used wood from *poumuli* trees to hold up a roof made of coconut leaves sewn together with rope. The rope was made of—you guessed it—coconut! They didn't use nails or glue. Everything they used to build the *fale* was local and natural. Some Samoans still build houses this way.

Fale in the Village

There are different kinds of *fale* in a traditional Samoan village. Many villages had a big meeting house. This big *fale* is for ceremonies and meetings. There's also a separate *fale* for cooking food. Most villages even have a *fale* for guests.

The Perfect Shelter

Did you notice that the *fale* has no walls? Can you guess why? It has to do with the weather. It can be very hot in the islands. The open shape of the *fale* keeps it cool inside. The breeze passes through the house. The roof provides shade and shelter from the rain.

The Roof

Here's one more fun fact about *fale*. Look at the design of the roof. It looks like an upside-down boat. Island boats were often built the same way as the roofs, using the same materials!

ISLAND CLOTHES

What kind of clothes did early Pacific Islanders like Moana wear? What about on special occasions? It depends on the island.

Tapa Cloth

Many early Pacific Islanders wore clothes made of tapa cloth. Fiji, Samoa, and Tonga were some of the places that made tapa. Tapa is made out of tree bark. Villagers softened the bark by soaking it in water and beating it. Often they would decorate the tapa with beautiful designs.

Special Occasions

During certain ceremonies, many Pacific Islanders wore headdresses. The headdresses were mostly made from plants, feathers, and shells from the island.

Weaving with coconut leaves

Use What You Have!

Pacific Islanders made everything they needed with what they had on the island. In Samoa, islanders created clothes from softened tree bark and wove clothes out of leaves. They decorated the clothing using dyes made from the nuts, seeds, juices, and sap of plants on the island.

EXPRESS YOURSELF!

Gramma Tala, Tui, and Moana don't just wear tapa. They wear necklaces too! What about Moana's friend Maui? He has tattoos. Let's look at some of the ways Pacific Islanders express themselves.

Jewelry

Some Pacific Islanders wear jewelry. Their ancestors made it out of local island material. Shells, bone, seeds, wood, and coconut were commonly used. Sometimes they would wear jewelry just for special ceremonies. Sometimes it was worn to show wealth or power. Some kinds of necklaces were worn only by chiefs.

Masks

On many Melanesian islands, people made masks. These would be worn during special ceremonies. In Papua New Guinea, only men wore masks. Some masks were made to be worn. Some were hung in houses or on the front of canoes.

Tattoos

On many Pacific Islands, tattoos were and still are a very important part of the culture. Samoans have been tattooing for more than two thousand years. Tattoos are done by hand using a tool made from a sharp tooth or a row of metal teeth. Tattooing a young man or woman is a special event. The tattoos are very painful. It is thought that getting tattooed shows you are brave.

ANCIENT WISDOM OF THE ISLANDS

The first Pacific Islanders made drawings, carvings, and statues. But they didn't think of them as just art. These objects were more than decoration. They often had ceremonial or religious meaning. They were created to help tell stories and remember special events.

The *Moai*

These are the *moai*. They are statues found on Rapa Nui. Rapa Nui is also called Easter Island. The moai were carved hundreds of years ago. The tallest statue is almost 33 feet (10 m) high! The moai may represent the ancestors of the sculptors.

Ha'amonga 'a Maui

This is a monument in Tonga called Ha'amonga 'a Maui. That means "Burden of Maui." The monument is made of three huge stone slabs. Each one weighs more than 40,000 pounds (18,000 kg)! It is almost a thousand years old. It may have been built to measure time using the sun.

Petroglyphs

Petroglyphs are rock drawings. The Marquesas Islands have many petroglyphs. There are drawings of turtles, canoes, and people. We have no idea how old they are.

MUSIC

Music is a big part of Moana's life. She first beat a drum when she was a little girl. A lot of Pacific Islanders think of music as a very important part of their cultures.

Pahu

Lali

Rattles

Drums!

In Polynesia, a drum called the pahu is made from coconut trees and sharkskin. In Fiji, lalis—long drums made from logs—are common. In Papua New Guinea, many musicians played rattles. These are made from seeds, leaves, and shells. Music was and still is a big part of many ceremonies and dances.

Singing!

Pacific Islanders have been singing for thousands of years. They sang as part of many religious ceremonies. Sometimes they used song to pass stories down from one generation to the next.

In the Pacific, songs have always been a way to document important events.

Instruments!

What other instruments are played in the Pacific Islands? Some Polynesians play the nose flute. Other islanders play conch shells or panpipes. In recent times, the guitar and ukulele have become popular instruments to use in Pacific Island music.

Nose flute

Conch shell

Panpipes

VILLAGE LIFE

Moana's father, Tui, is the chief of her village. What does it mean to be chief? What was it like living in a village like Moana's?

Village Chiefs

On many of the Pacific Islands, villages were made up of groups of families. The families are very close. In Samoa, each village is led by chiefs. Chiefs are in charge of their own families and all the other families in the village. The chiefs don't act alone. Everyone in the village helps make important decisions.

Ceremonies

A chief has a lot of responsibilities. One of them is leading village ceremonies. Each village is like its own country. Villages have lots of events on the *malae*, or village square. They can be religious ceremonies. Some events can be about problems villagers are having. They can also be weddings and celebrations.

Celebration in Vanuatu

Honored Guests

In Samoa, guests from other villages are welcomed with open arms. When guests arrive, the ceremonies begin. The chief or his children may put on a headdress or *tuiga* as part of a welcome ceremony. The women of the village march toward the guesthouse. They sing and dance while they do this. They bring the guests the best food they have. They give speeches, sing songs, and exchange gifts.

THE IMPORTANCE OF THE OCEAN

Why is the ocean so important to the people of the Pacific Islands? The ocean is a big part of everyday life. It is, in many ways, part of their home. It provides a source of food and a way to get around.

The Bounty of the Ocean

How did the Pacific Islanders find food in the ocean? Islanders fished with nets, baskets, and hooks. Sometimes they fished from shore, and sometimes they fished from boats. Some Samoan fishhooks were made from snail shells. Fish were and are a very important source of food for Pacific Islanders.

Canoes

The first Pacific explorers traveled on boats. They sailed thousands of miles on canoes. There are no canoes from that time left in the world. But new canoes exist that are similar. And we can make some guesses about what the early canoes were like. The most important boat for long trips was the double-hulled canoe. This canoe was built to make many long voyages.

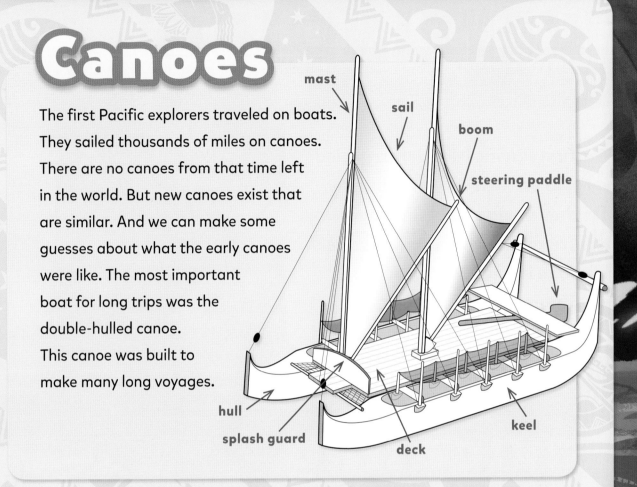

mast

sail

boom

steering paddle

hull

splash guard

deck

keel

The Great Connector

The Pacific Islands are spread out across the ocean. They are far from one another, and even farther from other parts of the world. It's easy to think that the ocean keeps the islands isolated. But that's not how the people of the Pacific Islands think. They see the ocean as the great connector. It connects the islands to one another. It connects the islands to the world.

WAYFINDING

The first Pacific Islanders traveled very far on their canoes. But how did they navigate, or find their way, across open ocean? Or from island to island? They practiced wayfinding!

Navigating Without Instruments

Early Pacific Islanders didn't have most of the tools that we have today to find our way. They didn't have compasses. They didn't have sextants, which are special instruments to measure distance. The earliest explorers didn't even have maps! So how did they do it? In Micronesia early explorers trained using a stick chart. The stick chart mapped where islands and currents were. Wayfinders used their eyes and ears and studied the ocean for years. They remembered what they learned and passed their knowledge on, often through song.

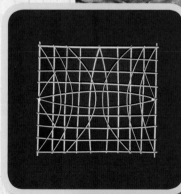

Currents, Waves, and Colors

Island voyagers used the ocean itself to find their way. They learned to recognize the changing ocean currents. They studied the speed and size of ocean waves. They even looked at the changing color of the ocean!

Red-billed tropic bird

Ocean Animals

The early voyagers watched traveling animals. They learned the flight paths of local birds. When the birds flew overhead, this gave them information. They watched for sea turtles and the direction they were traveling. They noticed how fast they were swimming. All of these were important clues to the wayfinders.

Green sea turtle

USING THE SKY TO GET AROUND

The first Pacific explorers didn't just look down at the ocean when they were wayfinding. They also looked up at the sky!

The Day Sky

Early Pacific Islanders realized that clouds move toward land in a special V shape. They also noticed that clouds changed color when they were over land. Clouds were brighter over a white sand beach. Clouds were darker over a forest or a black sand beach. Early wayfinders also used the sun to find their way. They knew that the sun rises in the east and sets in the west. That helped them know where they were going.

The Night Sky

Early voyagers didn't navigate only during the day. They also used the stars at night to find their way. Wayfinders watched the positions of the stars move in the sky. As stars rose and fell in the sky, wayfinders could tell which direction they were heading.

Watching the Wind

wind flag

Wayfinders paid close attention to the wind. Some of them made wind flags and tied them to their canoes. The flags, made of feather and bark, would point in the direction the wind was blowing.

Memory and Observation

Wayfinders had amazing memories. They had to memorize stars, wind patterns, wave shapes, ocean colors, currents, and more. Not only that— they had to pay attention all the time. They had to notice every change in the wind, the sky, and the ocean.

EARLY PACIFIC ISLANDERS AND EXPLORATION

We've learned that people didn't always live on the Pacific Islands. They traveled there! That's a long trip across the ocean. Let's learn more about these adventurous explorers.

Where Did They Come From?

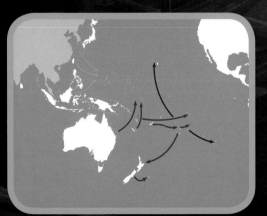

We have no remaining records written by the first Pacific Islanders. What we know comes from stories like Gramma Tala's. We've also learned from petroglyphs and songs, but we can't be sure about the details of the first explorers. We think that many thousands of years ago, they sailed from Southeast Asia. They settled in New Guinea. Much later, they sailed east to the other Pacific Islands.

The Journey

The journey east would have taken months. The wayfinders brought plants and animals with them. They brought whatever they needed to start a new life. They did not know what they would find.

A Long Pause

After thousands of years of exploration, early islanders took a long break from exploring. Just how long this break lasted is not known for sure. Some historians think it may have lasted as long as one thousand years. Why did early islanders stop sailing east? We don't know! We also don't know why they started again about two thousand years ago.

MAUI STORIES

Gramma Tala knows a lot of stories about the demigod Maui. Different islands have different stories about him.

Tongan Maui

The Tongans say that Maui carries the weight of the earth on his shoulders. When Maui sleeps and nods his head, it causes earthquakes!

Māori Māui

The indigenous, or native, people of New Zealand are called the Māori.
The Māori tell stories about Māui too. They say he had a magic fishhook.
He used this fishhook to pull the island of New Zealand up from the sea. The Māori give thanks to Māui for giving them their home.

Hawai'ian Maui

In Hawai'i, there are many legends about Maui. One says he caught the sun with a rope. He made it slow down so that the days would be longer. Another says he lifted up the sky with his arms! A third says that he discovered the secret of fire. He gave it to people so they could cook and stay warm.

MORE TALES FROM THE ISLANDS

Maui isn't the only god in the Pacific! There are many stories about other gods that are important to the people of the Pacific Islands, their cultures, and their stories.

Ocean Gods

In Hawai'i, people worshipped many gods. They called them akua. Maui is just one akua of many. There is also Kanaloa, god of the ocean. There is Kāne, god of creation, sunlight, and fresh water. There is Lono, god of farming and rain. Each akua is in charge of a different part of life.

Rangi and Papa

In New Zealand, the Māori told stories about the beginning of the world. In their stories, the world began with Rangi and Papa. Rangi is the father of the world. He is the sky. Papa is the mother of the world. She is the earth. In the beginning, Rangi and Papa held each other tight, and everything was dark.

Tāne

Rangi and Papa had many sons. One of them was Tāne. Tāne is the god of forests and birds. One day Tāne pushed his parents apart. Rangi stays in the sky. Papa stays on the earth. This is how life began. When Rangi misses Papa, he cries. His tears are the rain.

ISLAND CHALLENGES

The Pacific Islands are full of plants, animals, and people. They are also full of stories. Pacific Islanders have lived in their homes for thousands of years. At times, though, they face challenges.

Living in Harmony

Each of the Pacific Islands is like a small world. All parts of the ecosystem, including the plants, animals, and people, have to live together. It takes a special balance for everyone to be happy. People cut down trees to make *fale*. Animals eat plants. People feed the animals. It is important to think about all the living things in your small world.

Water

The Pacific Islands are surrounded by water. But you can't drink the ocean. People need clean fresh water to drink. Some islands don't have very much fresh water. Plants and animals need water too. Water is a precious resource.

Keeping the Ocean Stories Alive

Gramma Tala learned the stories she tells from her parents and her grandparents. She passes them on to Moana. Moana will one day pass them on to the next generation. These stories are an important part of what makes the Pacific Islands special. By telling stories to one another, we keep the stories alive!

GOODBYE FOR NOW!

We've learned so much about the Pacific Islands Moana and her friends call home. We know about wayfinding and the importance of music in the cultures of the Pacific Islands. And we've learned that the ocean is the great connector that bridges the islands to one another and to the world.

As they say in Samoa, Tahiti, and Fiji: *Tōfā! Nana! Moce!* In other words:

Goodbye! Come visit soon!

GLOSSARY

adaptation: the way an animal's behavior or part of its body has changed over time so it becomes better fitted to survive

aerodynamic: designed in such a way so as to move through the air in a smooth and fast way

aluminum: a strong and light silver metal commonly used in automobiles

amphibian: a kind of animal that can live on land and in the water

atmosphere: a thin layer of gases around a planet or star

aurora: the scientific name for the polar lights

axle: a pin or metal shaft around which two wheels rotate

blowhole: a hole on top of an ocean mammal's head that it uses for breathing

blubber: a thick layer of fat that keeps whales warm in the cold ocean

brake pad: a thin block of friction-producing material attached to a caliper that squeezes against both sides of a brake disc when the brakes are applied

brake shoe: a curved steel plate covered with a thin block of friction-producing material that pushes against the inside of a brake drum when the brakes are applied

caliper: the part of a disc brake that straddles both sides of the disc and clamps down on it when the brakes are applied

camouflage: the way an animal changes color or shape to blend in with its environment

camshaft: a steel rod that controls the valves of an engine to open and close at the right time

celestial body: an object in space

ceramic: a strong, hard material often used to replace steel in many engine parts

chassis: the frame of a vehicle, onto which the engine, axles, and wheels are mounted

climate: the usual weather in a place

coastal waters: the part of the ocean closest to land

cold-blooded: an animal whose blood is the same temperature as the air or water around it. Fish and reptiles are cold-blooded.

comet: a big ball of ice that orbits around a star and has a tail of gas and dust

composite: something that is created by mixing separate materials

constellation: a group of stars that form a shape in the sky

crankshaft: a long metal rod in an engine that converts the up-and-down motion of the pistons into a rotating motion that sends power to the driving wheels

crumple zone: an area on a car that is designed to absorb most of the force in an accident

distributor: a device in the ignition system that sends electricity to each spark plug at just the right time to ignite the air and fuel mixture in the cylinders

drive system: a system that transfers the power from an engine to the wheels

drivetrain: the mechanical system that takes the rotating power from the engine and sends it out to the driving wheels of a motorized vehicle

echinoderm: a family of ocean animals. The family includes the sea star, the sea urchin, and the sea cucumber. Many echinoderms have spiny skin.

echolocation: a way whales use sound to measure the location and shapes of things by using sound waves

eclipse: when an object in space moves into the shadow of another object

ecosystem: a habitat and every living creature within it

efficiency: doing or producing something without wasting energy, time, or materials

electron: a tiny speck of energy with a negative charge

endurance race: a very long race that tests the ability of a car to drive over a long period of time

equator: a line exactly halfway between the North Pole and the South Pole that circles Earth

equinox: a day when day and night are of equal length

exhaust: burned fuel created during the combustion process

exhaust valve: a valve that opens to let out the burned fuel

expand: to get bigger in size or force

fauna: all the animals in a place

filter feeder: an ocean animal that feeds by filtering water. Filter feeders suck in water and filter it past their gills. Then they eat whatever is left. Whale sharks are filter feeders.

fish: an animal without legs that lives its whole life in water. Fish are cold-blooded and use gills to breathe oxygen in water.

flora: all the plants in a place

fluke: the horizontal tail of a whale

food web: a map of all the different plants and animals in one habitat that shows what the plants and animals eat and what eats them

friction: the resistance to movement between two objects as they slide against each other

gear: a strong wheel with notches, or "teeth," that meshes with other gears to control the power from the engine to the wheels

gills: what water-breathing animals use to get oxygen out of water

grassland: land covered in grasses and not trees

Ha'amonga 'a Maui: a monument in Tonga

habitat: the place where an animal or plant lives

headdress: a ceremonial covering worn on the head

indigenous: originally living in a place

intake: the step (or stroke) when the piston slides to the bottom of the cylinder and the intake valve opens to let in air and fuel

intake valve: a valve that opens to allow the fuel-air mixture into the cylinder and closes during the compression and combustion strokes

intertidal zone: the zone between the tides where the water meets the land in the ocean

kelp: a kind of algae. Kelp is one of the fastest-growing life-forms on the planet.

light pollution: when lights on Earth are so bright that they make it hard to see stars in the night sky

magnetic field: the area around a magnet where you can feel the magnetic force

mammal: an animal that breathes air. Mammals are warm-blooded and have hair.

Melanesia: a group of western Pacific Islands that includes Fiji, Papua New Guinea, and the Solomon Islands

meteor: a meteoroid that burns and glows in Earth's atmosphere

meteorite: a meteoroid that lands on Earth's surface

meteoroid: a rock in space

Micronesia: a group of northwestern Pacific Islands that includes Kiribati and the Marshall Islands

midnight sun: when the sun is so high near the North Pole or South Pole that it is visible even at midnight

migration: a long journey that an animal makes every year

moai: one of more than nine hundred statues with large heads spread all over Rapa Nui

native: originally from a place

navigate: to find one's way from one place to another

non-native: brought to a place from somewhere else

Northern Hemisphere: the top half of Earth

North Pole: the most northern point on Earth

North Star: the star in the Northern Hemisphere that shows where the north celestial pole is. It is also called Polaris.

Oceania: another name for the Pacific Islands

open ocean: every part of the ocean that is offshore and not close to land

orbit: to move around an object in a circular path

petroglyph: a rock drawing

piston: a circular piece of metal that moves up and down inside a cylinder

pod: a group of whales

polar night: when the sun is so low near the North Pole or South Pole that it doesn't rise for more than twenty-four hours

Polynesia: a group of Pacific Islands that includes Hawai'i, New Zealand, and Samoa

predator: an animal that eats other animals

rain forest: a forest where it rains a lot

rally circuit: the course upon which a rally race is held

rotor: a thin wing or a blade that produces a downdraft of air to move a helicopter upward

seabird: a bird that feeds in the ocean

sea urchin: an ocean animal related to sea stars that has many spines. Some urchins feed on kelp.

shock absorber: a combination of springs and a fluid- or air-filled tube that is connected to each wheel of a vehicle to reduce the force of sudden bumps or uneven surfaces on a road

solar maximum: the time every eleven years when the sun's magnetic activity is the greatest

solar system: the sun and the planets, moons, and other objects that orbit around it

Southern Hemisphere: the bottom half of Earth

South Pole: the most southern point on Earth

spark plug: a device that supplies the electric spark to ignite the compressed air and fuel mixture at the top of the cylinder and make an explosion

spoiler: an air deflector that is sometimes placed under the front bumper or on the rear end of a car to help keep it stable when traveling at high speeds

straightaway: the straight part of a road or race course where a driver may be able to pick up speed or pass another car

stroke: the distance traveled by a piston from its highest to lowest point in a cylinder. Stroke also refers to any of the four steps in the piston's operation: intake, compression, combustion, and exhaust.

summer solstice: the longest day of the year. It is also the first day of summer in many countries.

tapa: a cloth made from wild hibiscus bark

tattoo: a permanent marking or drawing on the skin made by tapping tools that apply ink

traction: how well a car's spinning tires are able to grip the road or track without slipping

transmission: the part of a vehicle that uses various gears to transfer the power from the engine to the wheels

tread: the grooves on a tire that help it grip the road

tuiga: a ceremonial Samoan headdress

tundra: parts of the world that have no trees and are very cold

tuner: a car that has been changed, or modified, to increase performance

warm-blooded: an animal whose blood is always warm even if the air or water around it is cold. Mammals like whales and people are warm-blooded.

wayfinding: the technique developed by early Pacific Islanders to travel across the ocean

winter solstice: the shortest day of the year. It is also the first day of winter in many countries.

INDEX

PHOTO CREDITS

All photos are listed by page number from top to bottom.

Front cover: Borisoff/Shutterstock; RooM the Agency/Alamy Stock Photo; Jolanta Wojcicka/Shutterstock. Title page: Borisoff/Shutterstock; Shotshop GmbH/Alamy Stock Photo; PA Images/Alamy Stock Photo; Don Mammoser/Shutterstock. Table of contents: imageBROKER/Alamy Stock Photo; Andrey_Kuzmin/Shutterstock; Jolanta Wojcicka/Shutterstock. Back cover: Cultura Creative (RF)/Alamy Stock Photo; Jolanta Wojcicka/Shutterstock.

Chapter 1: 6–7 background: © Shotshop GmbH/Alamy Stock Photo. 7: © Netfalls/Alamy Stock Photo; © Steven Russell Smith/Alamy Stock Photo. 8–9 background: © Stocktrek Images, Inc./Alamy Stock Photo. 8: © ARV/Alamy Stock Photo. 10–11 background: © RooM the Agency/Alamy Stock Photo. 10: © J.R. Bale/Alamy Stock Photo. 11: © Stocktrek Images, Inc./Alamy Stock Photo. 12: © Jim Henderson/Alamy Stock Photo. 13: © Radius Images/Alamy Stock Photo; © Dimitar Todorov/Alamy Stock Photo; © Teemu Tretjakov/Alamy Stock Photo. 15: © Zoonar GmbH/Alamy Stock Photo; © Ivy Close Images/Alamy Stock Photo; © jbd30/Alamy Stock Photo. 16–17 background: © imageBROKER/Alamy Stock Photo. 17: © SOTK2011/Alamy Stock Photo; © Stocktrek Images, Inc./Alamy Stock Photo. 18–19 background: © Design Pics Inc/Alamy Stock Photo. 19: © Jim Keir/Alamy Stock Photo. 20–21 background: © Carole-Anne Fooks/Alamy Stock Photo. 21: © PhotoAlto sas/Alamy Stock Photo; © Radius Images/Alamy Stock Photo; © Kati Molin/Alamy Stock Photo; © Laszlo Podor / Alamy Stock Photo. 22–23 background: © Image Source/Alamy Stock Photo. 22: © imageBROKER/Alamy Stock Photo. 23: © Stocktrek Images, Inc./Alamy Stock Photo; © J.R. Bale/Alamy Stock Photo. 25: © Cultura Creative (RF)/Alamy Stock Photo. 26: © imageBROKER/Alamy Stock Photo. 27: © Joseph Gruber/Alamy Stock Photo. 28–29 background: © Cultura Creative (RF)/Alamy Stock Photo. 28: © RooM the Agency/Alamy Stock Photo. 29: © Gaetano Images Inc./Alamy Stock Photo. 30–31 background: © CVI Textures/Alamy Stock Photo. 30: © Deco/Alamy Stock Photo. 31: © Marvin Dembinsky Photo Associates/Alamy Stock Photo; © Science Photo Library/Alamy Stock Photo; © EpicStockMedia/Alamy Stock Photo. 32–33 background: © Stocktrek Images, Inc./Alamy Stock Photo. 32: © Artem Povarov/Alamy Stock Photo. 34–35 background: © Maksim Evdokimov/Alamy Stock Photo. 34: © Stocktrek Images, Inc./Alamy Stock Photo; © Elvele Images Ltd/Alamy Stock Photo. 35: © Stocktrek Images, Inc./Alamy Stock Photo. 36–37 background: © Angel Di Bilio/Alamy Stock Photo. 37: © Science Lab/Alamy Stock Photo. 38–39 background: © Radius Images/Alamy Stock Photo. 38: © Giulio Ercolani/Alamy Stock Photo. 39: © Dimitar Todorov/Alamy Stock Photo; © Daniel Dempster Photography/Alamy Stock Photo. 10–41 background: © Pere Sanz/Alamy Stock Photo. 40: © Stocktrek Images, Inc./Alamy Stock Photo. 41: © Stocktrek Images, Inc./Alamy Stock Photo. 42–43 background: © Adam Filipowicz/Alamy Stock Photo. 42: © imageBROKER/Alamy Stock Photo; © EyeEm Mobile GmbH/Alamy Stock Photo. 43: © imageBROKER/Alamy Stock Photo; © Jenna V. Genio/Alamy Stock Photo; © Image Source/Alamy Stock Photo.

Chapter 2: 46–47 background: Willyam Bradberry/Shutterstock. 47: Ethan Daniels/Shutterstock; worldswildlifewonders/Shutterstock; iliuta goean/Shutterstock. 48–49 background: Rich Carey/Shutterstock. 48: Krzysztof Odziomek/Shutterstock; JonMilnes/Shutterstock. 49: Krzysztof Odziomek/Shutterstock; Richard Whitcombe/Shutterstock. 50–51 background: Dudarev Mikhail/Shutterstock. 50: Miles Away Photography/Shutterstock. 51: Birdiegal/Shutterstock; Isabelle Kuehn/Shutterstock. 52–53 background: Willyam Bradberry/Shutterstock. 52: Sheri Armstrong/Shutterstock; Mikhail Blajenov/Shutterstock; mexrix/Shutterstock. 53: Longjourneys/Shutterstock; Yann Hubert/Shutterstock; Ivan Histand/Shutterstock. 54–55 background: Andrea Izzotti/Shutterstock. 54: NatalieJean/Shutterstock; Wildnerdpix/Shutterstock. 55: Joost van Uffelen/Shutterstock; Michael Cummings/Shutterstock. 56–57 background: Ethan Daniels/Shutterstock; Shane Gross/Shutterstock. 57: Willyam Bradberry/Shutterstock; WaterFrame/Alamy Stock

Chapter 1 was written by Paul Dichter with consultant Dr. Jessie Christiansen. Chapter 2 was written by Paul Dichter with consultant Ed Mastro, Exhibits Director, Cabrillo Marine Aquarium, San Pedro, CA. Chapter 3 was written by Larry Heiman with consultant Leslie Mark Kendall, Chief Curator at Petersen Automotive Museum, Los Angeles, CA. Chapter 4 was written by Paul Dichter with consultant Niuafolau Dionne Fonoti of the National University of Samoa.

Lerner Publications Company
A division of Lerner Publishing Group, Inc.
241 First Avenue North
Minneapolis, MN 55401 USA

For reading levels and more information, look up this title at www.lernerbooks.com.

Main body text set in Mikado.
Typeface provided by HVD Fonts.

Library of Congress Cataloging-in-Publication Data

The Cataloging-in-Publication Data for *The Magic of Our World: From the Night Sky to the Pacific Islands with Favorite Disney Characters* is on file at the Library of Congress.
ISBN 978-1-5415-4250-1 (pbk.)
ISBN 978-1-5415-4255-6 (eb pdf)

Manufactured in the United States of America
1-45415-39604-4/12/2018